Hare Krishna

STUDIES IN CONTEMPORARY RELIGIONS

Volumes in Print:

*Baha'i*
Margit Warburg

*The Church of Scientology*
J. Gordon Melton

*Hare Krishna*
Federico Squarcini & Eugenio Fizzotti

*Osho Rajneesh*
Judith M. Fox

*Soka Gakkai*
Karel Dobbelaere

*The Unification Church*
Massimo Introvigne

Additional volumes to follow.

# Hare Krishna

Federico Squarcini
and Eugenio Fizzotti

STUDIES IN CONTEMPORARY RELIGIONS

Massimo Introvigne, Series Editor

Signature Books
in cooperation with CESNUR
(Center for Studies on New Religions)

Cover design by Ron Stucki

Photographs courtesy of
Bhaktivedānta Book Trust International, Inc.



Published in the United States of America by Signature Books. Signature Books is a registered trademark of Signature Books Publishing, LLC.

www.signaturebooks.com

LIBRARY OF CONGRESS CATALOGING-IN-PUBLICATION DATA
Squarcini, Federico
[Gli Hare Krishna. English]
Hare Krishna by Federico Squarcini, Eugenio Fizzotti.
p. cm. — (Studies in contemporary religions ; 6)
ISBN 1-56085-168-6 (pbk.)
Includes bibliographical references.
1. International Society for Krishna Consciousness—United States. 2. Hare Krishnas—United States.
I. Fizzotti, Eugenio. II. Title.
III. Series.

BL1285.835.U6F59 2004
294.5'512—dc22

2004041746

# Contents

# 1.

# The Early History and Subsequent Phases

The Hare Krishna[1] movement began on July 13, 1966, when it was registered in New York state as the International Society for Kṛṣṇa Consciousness (hereafter ISKCON). Born of the single-minded effort of a solitary pioneer, it evolved into an inter-continental reality that today boasts three hundred temples and centers around the world, about forty rural communities, and many ISKCON-sponsored restaurants. In fact, it exists in almost every country and enjoys considerable international fame.

The early years were more precarious. When the founder arrived in the United States, he was already advanced in age, and he spent a difficult first year in loneliness, then dwelt in a tiny apartment on Manhattan's lower east side surrounded by a handful of aspiring young disciples. But his endeavors were rewarded when these young people took his message to heart and began proselytizing. The movement expanded quickly across the country.

The frenetic pace of expansion created difficulties for future historians who now face a dearth of documentation for some aspects of the early period. In addition, the growth was uncoordinated, dependent on local cultural and organizational demands, and unsynchronized.[2] In each area where ISKCON operated, its history should be treated separately because of the specific circumstances and undeniable differences in each region. One can identify overall trends, but to generalize is to overlook the uniqueness of the various trajectories. However, for the purposes of this book, these complexities will have to be mentioned only briefly.

How many Hare Kṛṣṇas are there in the world? No one has conducted a precise census.[3] The difficulty is not in a reluctance by ISKCON members to be counted, but in determining what constitutes membership. In the beginning, when members were cloistered, it would have been easy to count the residents, but today adherents are classified variously as "initiated resident members," "uninitiated resident members," "initiated non-resident members," and "uninitiated non-resident members" according to an individual's degree of commitment and participation in the movement.[4]

The founder referred to believers simply as "devotees." His followers continued to refer to each other with the same expression, but the condition of being a devotee has not always implied an ontological status; it has been a shifting notion that has been influenced by different nuances.[5] Initially only residents of temple compounds—those who strictly followed the rules and customs of a cloistered life—were devotees. The designation expanded to include former temple residents when they began moving out of the temple compounds to begin families but still observed the principles of the creed. Individuals who had never joined a temple but had adapted their habits to create a temple atmosphere within their households also came to be considered devotees.

This was the state of things until outside members began to lose a sense of belonging, absent the compelling social control of the temple community. In addition, compromises had to be made in order to survive in the external world. It seemed inappropriate to designate people as devotees who, despite a devotional past, had become "corrupted" by a "material life," so the expression "external devotee" was coined for such individuals. Instead of being simply descriptive, the term belied an indifference and occasional diffidence between temple residents and those who lived on the outside.[7]

Despite the difficulties in determining what constitutes true membership, it is possible to estimate a current worldwide population of about 10,000 resident devotees. With regard to external adherents, now referred to by ISKCON as "congregational members," there are about 400,000.[8] Based on other criteria, the figures would be greater or less for either category, but the composite would remain about the same. Even so, any enumeration must be tied to the internal changes in classification that have paralleled the prevailing trends in each historical phase of the movement. Hence, a knowledge of ISKCON's history is important in understanding the subtleties of demographics.

The history of a movement usually begins with a consideration of the founder's life. In this case, the founder's history *is* ISKCON's history because of the central role he played —and continues to play—in the movement he created.

## THE FOUNDER

Abhay Caran De was the founder of the Hare Kṛṣṇa movement. He was initiated into the *saṇnyāsa* (those who renounce the world) as Bhaktivedānta Svāmī. Later he would become better known by the honorific title of Śrīla Prabhupāda.[9] He was born in Calcutta on September 1, 1896. According to his hagiography, his family belonged to the

Gauḍīya Vaiṣṇava tradition.[10] Gauḍīya refers to the ancient territory of Gauda and Vaiṣṇava indicates worship of the Hindu god Viṣṇu. As a young man, he studied in Calcutta at the Scottish Churches' College, which had been founded a century earlier by the Christian missionary, Alexander Duff.

In 1918 Abhay followed his father's recommendation and married Rādhārāṇī Datta. In 1920 he completed the required curriculum for a B.A. diploma but refused to receive it in protest of the British occupation of India and in a show of sympathy with Mohandas Gandhi.[11] When he completed his studies, Abhay apprenticed with a small pharmaceutical company. Later he would develop his own independent line of pharmaceuticals.

In 1922 Abhay was invited by a friend to hear an itinerant ascetic deliver a public speech. He was reluctant at first but finally agreed to hear the *sādhu*, as such preachers were called. The *sādhu* that day was Bhaktisiddhānta Sarasvatī (1874-1937), who had a profound effect on Abhay and was to be his future spiritual master.[12] Already during this first encounter, Bhaktisiddhānta asked Abhay to devote his life to preaching the message of Caitanya Mahāprabhu[13] in western countries.

The request left a strong impression on the young man's heart. From that day on, the proposal would remain alive in his thoughts, although it would be a very long time before he fulfilled the commission. In the meantime, he began visiting the guru regularly until, on November 21, 1932, in the northern Indian city of Allahabad, Abhay became initiated as his disciple. As part of the ceremony, his name was changed to Abhay Charanaravinda, he was taught how to chant Kṛṣṇa's holy names according to the Gauḍīya custom, and he was granted the status of brahmanhood—receiving the *yajñopavīta* thread traditionally worn by Brahmans. In addition, he received the *gāyatrī mantra*,[14] a sacred formula whispered into the disciple's ear by his master.[15] The fact that Abhay was considered eligible for brahmanhood indicates the progressive nature of Bhaktisiddhānta's theology. Priestly duties and the privilege of pursuing textual studies were generally available only to men who were born into the Brahman caste.[16] Abhay's master disavowed such dogmas, including the penalty of caste deprivation for a guru who traveled outside of India or the stringent social ties enjoined by traditional monastic orders.[17]

On the first day of January 1937, Bhaktisiddhānta died in Jagannath ͅPurī, a holy city southwest of Calcutta. Soon thereafter, his followers began to quarrel among themselves about who would succeed him as leader of the Gauḍīya-maṭha, his brand of Hinduism.[18] A few weeks prior to his master's demise, Abhay engaged him in a final epistolary exchange, at which time the guru reiterated his exhortation of 1922: "I have every hope that you can turn yourself into a very good English preacher."[19]

Abhay kept aloof from his Gauḍīya-maṭha colleagues, although he contributed to the movement financially and intellectually. In 1939 he was publicly honored with the title of Bhaktivedānta to acknowledge his erudition and spiritual clarity. During this period, he wrote articles to promulgate the teachings of Caitanya Mahāprabhu and Hindu scripture, particularly the *Bhagavad-gītā*. In Calcutta in February 1944, he founded the magazine, *Back to Godhead,* as a spiritual alternative to the socio-political problems tormenting India at the time.[20] He single-handedly wrote, edited, printed, and distributed this newspaper throughout the country for several years despite the wartime hardships, not the least of which was the rationing of newsprint.

Abhay's business had developed into a full-fledged pharmaceutical firm with a full line of products and a distinctive brand name. However, because of the difficult postwar economic realities, he had to close his factory in Lucknow in 1948 and restrict himself to a small pharmacy in Allahabad.

Two years later, he resolved to withdraw altogether from business and family affairs and devote himself completely to spiritual pursuits, still mindful of his guru's advice. Publication of *Back to Godhead* had been temporarily suspended, but it was resumed in 1952, although again single-handedly.

On May 16, 1953, Bhaktivedānta founded the League of Devotees in Jhansi, Madhya Pradesh. He wanted it to be a religious brotherhood that would spread Gauḍīya Vaiṣṇava beliefs and practices. He initiated his first disciple that same year. However, no real support materialized and the League of Devotees proved to be short-lived.[21]

In September 1956 Bhaktivedānta moved to Vṛndāvana, a major pilgrimage site in northern India, so he could begin an intense study and translation of Hindu scriptures. On September 17, 1959, he resolved to take the *saṇnyāsa* vows and renounce all material goods and family bonds, to consecrate himself fully to a spiritual life. He was renamed A. C. Bhaktivedānta Svāmī. Now he would direct all his energies toward planning a journey to the West.

First, he began translating the *Bhāgavata-purāṇa*, the foremost Sanskrit classic within the tradition of *Kṛṣṇa-bhakti* (devotion to Kṛṣṇa). He completed the first of twelve cantos in three parts and had them printed in 1962, 1964, and 1965. He knew that these would be an important resource in the diffusion of international awareness of Kṛṣṇaism.[22]

At the venerable age of sixty-nine, he contemplated the charge that Bhaktisiddhānta had given him thirty years earlier and asked a pious Hindu woman, Sumati Morarji, who owned the Scindia shipping lines, to grant him a complimentary passage to America. After persistent efforts, she agreed to give him a free ticket. A few days before the scheduled departure, he traveled to Calcutta with very little in the way of personal luggage. However, he did bring a large inventory of his recent publications. Scant notice was given of his departure beyond noting, in a small local newspaper, the *Dainik Basumati,* that he had embarked on a voyage to the United States. On August 13, 1965, at 9:00 A.M., he sailed from Calcutta on the merchant ship *Jaladuta,* headed for Boston and New York.

The crossing was difficult for the aged swami, as documented in his diary. He suffered two serious heart attacks over the thirty-five days of the journey.[23] Nevertheless, he walked on foreign soil for the first time on September 17, 1965, at 5.30 A.M., as he strolled the byways of Boston harbor. After a short layover, he took up the voyage again, continuing on to New York City and his new life.

He remained in Manhattan only briefly before continuing on to Butler, Pennsylvania, where Mr. and Mrs. Gopal and Sally Agarwal awaited him. Gopal's father had sent an advance letter of introduction on behalf of the swami. Yet, Bhaktivedānta could not remain long, sequestered in a small town. After a month of acclimatization, he moved back to New York City and called on Dr. Rāmamūrti Miśra, director of a yoga center situated next to Central Park. Dr. Miśra's name had been passed on to the swami by a common acquaintance in Bombay.

What he found in Manhattan was the counter-cultural movement of the 1960s, then in progress.[24] Most likely, he would not have fully grasped the implications of these circumstances. He only knew that he needed to design a strategy to spread Kṛṣṇa devotion in a way that would be in harmony with his master's teachings.[25]

His problem was that he lacked the basic economic means for survival and was therefore forced to improvise with makeshift accommodations, moving frequently from one apartment to another. The chance of staying permanently in the United States was becoming more remote.

He recorded his experiences in his private diary, of which the following is typical for this period: "There was no response of the visitors invited to come and join Hari Kirtan [singing of Hari's name] this evening at 7:30 p.m. But I alone executed the Kirtan ceremony with my T. R. [tape recorder] till 10 p.m."[26] He persevered: "According to Māyāpur-Panjika [a Bengali calendar], today is Adhivas day of Gour Purnima [the most important Gauḍīya Vaiṣṇava celebration]. Devotees at Vrindaban and Nabadwipa are enjoying the celebration. I am here alone without any devotee companion. But I have come here to serve the Lord and not for personal happiness. I am prepared to live in hell even if I am able to serve the Lord. Sri Chaitanya Mahaprabhu wanted that His mission should be propagated all over the world and that is my objective. I do not mind the inconvenience personally felt."[27]

He moved to the Lower East Side in mid-1966 between Little Italy and Chinatown, where his endurance would bear fruit on June 12 when he prepared a feast for sixteen young guests. To the great delight of these young people, the meal included twelve traditional Bengali dishes. The convivial atmosphere was so successful that Sunday feast became a regular preaching tool from then on. On July 1, with help from some of the young people he had met, he rented a small shop on Second Avenue called Matchless Gifts and began lecturing on the *Bhagavad-gītā* before a growing audience.[28]

In retrospect, the most important event of this period was, no doubt, the less visible but historic submission of legal documents to register the International Society for Krishna Consciousness (ISKCON) on July 13.[29] On September 8, he held his first ISKCON initiation ceremony for eleven candidates. In the fall the ISKCON Press would be inaugurated.

The young people he met found themselves charmed beyond measure by the exotic clothes and behavior of this elderly Calcutta gentleman. Gradually, his circumstances began to reverse themselves. His acquaintances were so intrigued by his public chanting and total devotion to Kṛṣṇa that they became constant companions.[30] More and more sympathizers joined him, and over time these young people became full disciples. They, in turn, traveled to other cities to open new centers and recruit more members.[31]

A handful of his disciples relocated to San Francisco in 1966 to found a west coast temple. To reinforce their spirit, the swami joined them in mid-January 1967 in time for one of the main countercultural events of the era, the Mantra Rock Dance. In the summer of the next year, another important episode in ISKCON history occurred, the first public Cart Festival (*Ratha-yātrā*),[32] held on the streets of San Francisco. The festival would become an important instrument in diffusing Kṛṣṇa consciousness from Los Angeles to Tokyo; it remains an annual ISKCON custom in many countries.

From the earliest days in New York, Bhaktivedānta's disciples had addressed him as *Svāmīji*, but in May 1968 in Boston, one of his disciples suggested the honorific epithet that Bhaktivedānta had used for his guru, Bhaktisiddhānta. He agreed and was soon known as Śrīla Prabhupāda.[33]

Bhaktivedānta's disciples opened the first rural community in the hills of West Virginia in the spring of 1968. They believed that in the natural environment, the swami's ideals could come to life through the integration of his profound spiritual message with the purity of a "simple" life. This idea, which is prevalent in Bhaktivedānta's writings, has been expressed in the slogan: "Simple living, high thinking."[34]

As the movement flourished in the United States, Bhaktivedānta dispatched three couples in July 1968 to export the religion to London, marking the beginning of ISKCON's world-wide expansion.[35] In the space of just a few years, Bhaktivedānta would be propelled from organizer of the first local activities in New York City to an ever-increasing itinerary of world-wide preaching tours. Even when facing health problems from 1967 to 1972, he still traveled and preached. In July 1967 he returned to India; two years later he visited Europe to preach in England and Germany; he went to India again in 1970; traveled the next year to Australia, Kenya, Russia, and Hawaii; and returned to Honolulu to preach again in 1972.

Adherents assumed the traits for which they would become known in the public mind as they appropriated distinctive Indian dress and customs (see chapter 2). They became strict lacto-vegetarians, eating only consecrated food (*prasāda*), and performed their liturgy publicly as devotional chants (*kīrtana, bhajana*), accompanied by traditional Indian drums and cymbals. They imported increasing quantities of musical instruments from the subcontinent. All of this branded the movement and enhanced its appeal for many converts.[36]

As the demands on Bhaktivedānta's time increased, he recognized the necessity of creating what he called the Governing Body Commission (GBC), conceived on July 28, 1970, with positions filled by twelve senior devotees. These twelve were to assume the worldwide administration of ISKCON.[37] The Bhaktivedānta Book Trust publishing company was also founded at this time, although it would be two years before it was officially registered.[38] The book trust was to be governed by a board of trustees and entrusted with the supervision of the production and distribution of all of Bhaktivedānta's writings. Soon thereafter, Bhaktivedānta sought a network of financial sponsors for special projects. In August 1970 in Calcutta, he initiated Indian sponsors into the ISKCON Life Membership program. This group is still active today, both in India and among the Indian diaspora who live abroad.

These dramatic developments were not without difficulties and contradictions. On several occasions, the master had to intervene to settle managerial disputes and quarrels among the leadership, as evidenced by the recorded polemics over some unorthodox approaches to book distribution,[39] misunderstandings about the character of the guru in the New Vrindavana community in West Virginia,[40] the problem of disciples consulting Indian masters,[41] the perceived insubordination of Bhaktivedānta's disciple Siddhasvarūpa,[42] and conflicts between celibate and married disciples.[43] In each case, Bhaktivedānta raised his voice or insisted in some other authoritarian way that his view would prevail and the controversy would be resolved. In 1972 he temporarily froze the administrative power of the GBC altogether.[44]

The peak in creativity and growth occurred in the mid-1970s. At that time, circulation of Bhaktivedānta's literature was brisk, and the organization was buying real estate around the world for temples and centers.[45] Bhaktivedānta's core works were released in the first half of the 1970s, including a complete edition of the *Bhagavad-gītā* (*Bhagavad-*

*gītā as It Is*) published by Collier-Macmillan; the trilogy *Kṛṣṇa: The Supreme Personality of Godhead,* prefaced by George Harrison; the massive *Śrīmad-bhāgavatam*;[46] and the Bengali work *Caitanya-caritāmṛta* in seventeen volumes. In 1971 and 1972, Bhaktivedanta took part in laying the cornerstones for three ambitious ISKCON projects in India: the Māyāpur Chandrodāyā Mandir in West Bengal; Hare Kṛṣṇa Land in Mumbai (Bombay); and the Kṛṣṇa-Balarām Mandir at Vṛndāvana, a city in the Indian state of Uttar Pradesh.

From 1975 to 1977, the swami's activities became even more intense. In addition to the demanding work of translation and his correspondence load, he took up the task of visiting the growing communities (seventy-six in 1975) around the world in order to inspire followers with his message of devotion to Kṛṣṇa.[47] When all was said and done, he was still the real leader of the movement, the only spiritual counselor, the only true manager, and the last word on matters of importance.[48]

He curtailed travel plans in 1977 due to ill health and spent the last few months of his life in Vṛndāvana, India, the holiest site of Gauḍīya Vaiṣṇavism. His demise occurred on November 14, 1977, at 7:20 P.M. Left behind were roughly 5,000 initiated disciples, thousands of sympathizers, about a hundred centers throughout the world, impressive temples, and a deep and burdensome spiritual legacy.

## THE FIRST PHASE

### From Focus on the Founder to the Monopoly of the Sacred

The founder of ISKCON played the leading role in the history of the movement, but his demise left a stage filled with heterogeneous characters from around the world. It is perhaps inevitable that when a charismatic leader dies, some previously concealed disagreements will emerge.[49] In this case, the founder's last official statement regarding succession gave the managerial and political authority to the Governing Body Commission, while tutelage of ISKCON's world assets was given to various boards of trustees.[50] The matter of spiritual authority was more vague.

On July 9, 1977, Bhaktivedānta signed a letter prepared for him by his secretary that was one of the last documents he would produce. In it, he authorized eleven *ṛtviks* (officiators) to perform initiation ceremonies during his absence due to illness. The guidelines implied that the eleven were, as his direct disciples, representatives and not successors.[51] However, other documents—transcriptions of tape-recorded statements and an emending codicil related to the testament of June 4, 1977[52]—seemed to confer more power and autonomy on these representatives.[53] To outsiders, the variations appear to be subtle, but to insiders, the ambiguities produced grave consequences. To this day, scholars have tried without success to unravel the founder's intentions, with no definitive explanation for the discrepancies yet emerging.[54]

After the swami's death, the gurus appointed by the July 9 letter and related documents entered into a struggle with the remaining seven members of the GBC. The commission had been increased to eighteen members in March 1977. Within the GBC, the eleven monopolized deliberations and ultimately leadership of ISKCON because of their dual roles as initiating masters and members of the governing body. In brief, they simultaneously controlled both the secular and spiritual spheres of activity.[55] They shared another bond through the "Ācārya Committee," which they founded in 1978 to resolve issues related to guruship, particularly the appointment of new gurus.[56]

Initially, GBC members were allotted a geographical area of the world over which they were allowed to exercise a kind of political and managerial supervision. The territorial control increased the depth of the eleven gurus' influence, and the combination of secular and spiritual roles contributed to an autocratic rule. Before long, these gurus oversaw every aspect of their adherents' lives. New recruits fell under their complete jurisdiction. Furthermore, even direct disciples of Bhaktivedānta Svāmī who were Governing Body Commissioners, but not gurus, progressively submitted to the eleven.[57]

The conflict became palpable. As one author documented it: "[T]he guru lives on in his teachings even after his body is gone. But who is to be the final authority in interpreting the founder's teachings and their intentions? Who are the real inheritors of Prabhupāda's mantle? The new gurus? The Governing Body Commission? All the disciples of Prabhupāda who have the capacity to be gurus? No easy answers emerged in the years following Prabhupāda's death."[58]

Despite these perplexities, the model that was promoted by the eleven masters prevailed. They defined themselves as *ācāryas,* or those who know and teach good behavior, a title that formerly had been reserved only for the founder. The overlap of secular and religious power resulted in a structure known as the *zonal ācārya system* whereby the world was partitioned into regions over which these figures freely operated. They determined their own policies, economic strategies, and religious structure. A zonal guru was the sole "divine" intermediary within his area. He bore the responsibility for catalyzing faith and overseeing the spiritual progress of new adherents. This had the collateral effect of seeming to elevate the eleven *ācāryas* above Bhaktivedānta himself. In light of the *ācāryas'* new, absolute authority to act and interpret doctrine without reference to precedent, Bhaktivedānta's position was thus minimized. As the eleven *ācāryas* amassed greater deference from their followers, the GBC ratified a ceremony of daily worship (*guru-pūjā*) devoted to them. This rite was performed at the feet of the guru, or alternately before a photograph of him, sitting on a richly embellished throne similar to the founder's throne (*vyāsāsana*) which was the focal point in temple statuary.[59]

These were not matters of mere personalities or administrative styles. They reflected a more serious underlying issue of charismatic administration. The question was whether the traditional guru theology could be integrated within a democratic model.[60] How could the religion conciliate and systematize, within a polycentric institutional and international model, the spiritual master's traditional stature? How could a role such as the guru's, traditionally considered absolute, be subjected to board resolutions, ethics controls, and injunctions for doctrinal harmony? And how could the guru, who is by definition an inspired, charismatic, and autocratic figure and whose dictates are irrevocable and unquestionable, be piloted by an institution in the matter of instructing his own disciples? After all, followers are drawn to the guru by his charisma, an embodied expression of the divine as manifested through a guru's preaching.

History contains repeated examples of the clash between charismatic personalities and bureaucratic control. For ISKCON, the first public rift in this area occurred in early 1980 when the GBC felt compelled to suspend three gurus for one year each due to improper behavior.[61] Specifically, the charges were misuse of power, use of drugs, illegal possession of weapons, and the claim to be the sole successor and possible connection to Bhaktivedānta.[62] The GBC's move was unprecedented: an institutionalized and democratic commission had dared to discipline leaders who traditionally were considered beyond suspect or judgment. The formerly unassailable and transcendent position of the guru was irrevocably compromised by this event, and it would be cited in the future as grounds for other reconsiderations.

As courageous as the move was, it was initially ineffective[63] because the gurus pushed back with the full weight of their considerable influence to see that the action against them was revoked. They reasserted their position of absolute preeminence with support from an Indian master and godbrother of the founder who exerted his own pressure on the Governing Body Commission.

Nevertheless, the discovery of moral and spiritual limitations in the gurus tainted their authority and produced dissatisfaction among adherents. One of the eleven, presiding over the western zone of the United States, pushed for a redefinition of what a guru is and the restoration of Bhaktivedānta above subsequent masters. He removed his own throne from the temple room and suspended the worship ceremony addressed to him. However, he failed to win the support of other gurus.

Many of Bhaktivedānta's disciples knew that the Governing Body Commission was extremely important to him. They also knew what had become of the institution founded by Bhaktivedānta's master, Bhaktisiddhānta: after his death in 1937, his followers had failed to implement their guru's recommendation for a similar governing board and had tried instead to elect a single successor, with dire results.[64]

It was at this delicate moment that a new entity—a "third force," as it has been called—gained in self-esteem: it was the elite of Bhaktivedānta's disciples who had themselves held responsible positions within ISKCON but were neither gurus nor Governing Body Commissioners.[65] This group outnumbered the GBC and was closer to the local population within temples and communities than the commissioners; thus, it became the impetus in preparing the ground for the reform movement of 1984-1987, later called the "guru-reform movement."

During the annual meetings in India in March 1981, the GBC passed a resolution sanctioning its own ultimate authority over the gurus. The need seemed acute due to the scandals involving some of the gurus or what was more politely expressed as the declining credibility of the *ācāryas*. Yet, many still professed belief that charisma is genuine and organic and grounded in demonstrable spiritual qualities rather than in confirmation by arbitrary appointment.

The idea of the "self-evident guru" developed out of this debate. According to this thesis, enlightened guides whom god empowers to dispel the darkness of nescience cannot be democratically or bureaucratically appointed. The term "myth of appointment" emphasized that the mantle of authority is independent of board resolutions and institutions; it descends charismatically from a previous guru and is clearly recognizable in the exercise of spiritual qualities.

Another school of thought proffered that gurus should be organized as a board and increased in number. This was because of the spiritual shallowness displayed by some of the eleven. A solution of some kind was necessary lest Bhaktivedānta Svāmī be imputed with an incautious trust. It was proposed that all adherents could become gurus if they followed the path of purification outlined by Bhaktivedānta, a method that was genuine and infallible if strictly followed. This idea ultimately prevailed as the theoretic assumption behind the reform of the mid-1980s. For many of Bhaktivedānta's disciples, the door to guruship was now open.

Incidentally, these diverse readings of the "transmission

of charisma" contributed to the *ṛtvik-vāda* doctrine, the idea of an appointed officiator-guru. This concept sparked debate already in the late 1980s and grew to be even more controversial from 1995 to the present. Nonetheless, some of the current ISKCON leaders saw the rejection of the *single ācārya system* in favor of a board structure as a necessary "modernization" that gave up an "archaic form of organization."[66]

In April 1982 ISKCON experienced its first schism when it appointed three new gurus,[67] bringing the number to fourteen. One of the original eleven responded by seeking recognition from an elderly godbrother of Bhaktivedānta as the official guru of ISKCON. The GBC denounced this attempted coup, and Jayatirtha Svāmī and a few hundred of his disciples came out in open opposition to the main governing body of the movement. The GBC had no other choice but to expel him.[68] This took the membership completely by surprise: ISKCON was publicly confronted by a common "enemy," Bhaktivedānta's godbrother, who was from the outside and was backing an ex-guru against the authority of the founder.[69]

This turmoil resurfaced the next year at the annual meetings of March 1983. The remaining thirteen masters, apparently motivated by heartfelt self-criticism, approved a dramatic change of direction. They symbolically relinquished their thrones and endorsed a resolution to extend to all members of the GBC the eligibility to become gurus. One more guru was suspended from office a year later during a GBC meeting in Miami Beach, charged with drug use and insubordination.[70] That signaled the end to an era: unbridled charisma would not be countenanced, but neither would an attempt to impose a rigid institutionalization and standardization of Bhaktivedānta's charisma.

To counterbalance the tainted reputation resulting from such scandals, the public relations department tried to portray a more positive image by publicizing the movement's cultural roots and its constructive outlook. In Detroit, ISKCON purchased and renovated a prestigious estate, the Fisher Mansion, and converted it into an elegant cultural center and museum. The inauguration day in 1983 attracted wide media coverage and praise from state legislators.[71] In Italy and elsewhere in Europe, outdoor celebrations and festivals were held. ISKCON promoted another enterprise in 1983,[72] the humanitarian Food for Life program, which is still active in many areas of the world.

Despite these efforts, it was still an unlucky year for ISKCON. First, a resident of New Vṛndāvana in West Virginia was murdered. In a preliminary hearing on the West Coast, ISKCON was ordered to pay $32.5 million for recruiting an underage male who briefly joined the movement. In northern Europe, a guru who had been preaching in the Soviet Union was accused of espionage. Such incidents revived misgivings about the religion in American newspapers.[73]

In response to the hierarchical changes after Bhaktivedānta's death, many adherents became disillusioned and left the movement. Only about 1,000 were active by 1983 out of an original 5,000. Those who remained were joined by thousands of new adherents who had been converted by the zonal gurus. The total number of ISKCON communities was about two hundred worldwide, with about fifty in the United States.

Real reform took root in America at the end of 1984. Members committed themselves to relaunching the society with renewed loyalty to the founder's integrity and purity. This would be possible only if the internal structure of

ISKCON could be renovated, in particular where there were still vestiges of the *zonal ācārya system*. It became vital to the religion's image that all members, including the gurus, adhere strictly to the prescribed spiritual practices.[74]

The organizational transformation was augmented by impressive temple construction programs. When the grand Temple of Understanding was inaugurated in Durban, South Africa, in 1985, the event was attended by the highest dignitaries in the country. At the same time, leaders of the New Vṛndāvana community in West Virginia announced plans to build a colossal temple that would take ten years to compete and would cost sixty million dollars. The ISKCON centers in Europe reached a peak of activity as they continued to sponsor huge outdoor festivals. Such events resulted in positive press coverage, which in turn influenced the general public and helped to arouse enthusiasm among believers themselves.

## THE SECOND PHASE
### From Autocracy to Collegiality

The guru reform movement attracted the attention of the rank and file in 1984. The impetus for this was a September meeting of thirty-five North American temple presidents, regional secretaries, and non-guru *sannyāsins* who discovered, as they reviewed routine matters, that they shared a consensus about the changes they felt should be implemented within ISKCON. They stayed a month longer than planned to compile a reform document addressed to the North American Governing Body Commission.[75] This, along with protests elsewhere, spawned debate that engaged different factions, which for their part conducted surveys and produced documents that eloquently expressed the points of view of their constituencies.

This leaven of reform animated the epochal meetings of August and September 1985 at New Vṛndāvana. The regional guru who resided at New Vṛndāvana read a counter-reform document[76] and stormed out of the meeting. The North American temple presidents, trustees, and local managers (the "third force") and some of the North American Governing Body Commission members continued to refine their list of proposals in preparation for the annual GBC meetings scheduled for March 1986, a year that was ripe with meaning: it would be the five-hundred-year anniversary of the birth of Caitanya Mahāprabhu.

The GBC wanted to see the number of gurus increase to decentralize the influence of their spiritual leadership. The formerly unassailable monopoly of the *ācāryas* was beginning to give way. In early 1985, four new gurus were elected, bringing the total to fifteen.[77] According to proposals made in September 1985, the guruship would be opened to an even larger number of members. However, the procedural legitimacy of those meetings was not officially recognized.[78] Even so, the number of initiating gurus grew by the addition of nine new masters, then eleven more during the annual meetings of March 1986, and finally by six more who were identified as eligible candidates for 1987.[79]

The GBC asked the gurus to show goodwill by removing or lowering their thrones and introducing new criteria for the election of future gurus. Next, the GBC took the very concrete step in breaking up the zonal monopoly by allowing gurus to circulate freely in areas formerly reserved for the *ācāryas*.[80]

In the process of reform, Bhaktivedānta was restored to his position of primary spiritual authority[81] and was acknowledged as the *founder ācārya* and foundation for every initiative within the movement. He was the flag around which the scattered feudal groups of the *zonal ācārya system* could rally and reunite. The reformers were not altogether homogeneous, and it would be shown that they too harbored some extremists and self-interested individuals among their ranks.[82]

As the guru of the New Vṛndāvana community offered continued resistance,[83] another setback came from Europe where many of the local leaders, perhaps influenced by anti-Americanism, supported two reactionary gurus in charge of the northern and southern areas of the continent.[84] The gurus fostered a climate of non-cooperation, choosing to regard reform as a hindrance to good progress through preaching. In meetings in France in November 1985 and January 1986, they drafted counter proposals intended to hinder the reform.

Elsewhere, the picture was not so different: disciples of the new gurus, along with Bhaktivedānta's original disciples who were well integrated in the *zonal ācārya system,* were united against reform, while others of Bhaktivedānta's disciples and the non-aligned members favored it.

Yet, the year 1986 proved to be one of crisis for the gurus. Five of the eleven accepted reform. Two others had already been expelled for doctrinal reasons, and three disgraced themselves by engaging in illicit sexual behavior and left their vows,[85] while another who could not accept reform preferred to disassociate from ISKCON altogether.[86] This engendered a momentous transition. With the rise of a new generation of gurus on the one hand and the decline of the old *guru ācāryas* on the other, there was now little impediment to more radical change.

At meetings in Chicago in November 1986, the reformers elaborated their plans.[87] A year later, in March 1987 in Māyāpur, a new era had begun: for the first time, ten years after the founder's death, the entire movement paused long enough to review its progress and seriously ponder its future. The meetings lasted about three weeks, during which time—through unusually lengthy sessions—the deeds and character of each of the seventeen GBC members were scrutinized and judged by the external assembly of fifty individuals appointed by the GBC itself. No one was beyond suspicion. The organization determined that it was going to prevail over charisma once and for all.

The most notable official decisions to come out of the Māyāpur meetings were as follows:

a. The word *ācārya* would be strictly reserved for Bhaktivedānta, the only real *acāryā* and founder of ISKCON; this significant decision explicitly embodied the will to withdraw the disproportionate power earlier given to the founder's successors.

b. The GBC agreed to elect fifteen new commissioners, mostly reform leaders.

c. The GBC ratified the appointment of the gurus who had been elected over the previous two years and selected thirteen additional candidates.

d. The public worship of gurus was forbidden. Only the throne devoted to the founder's statue would be allowed in ISKCON temples. Other thrones were banned.

e. The standards of guru worship were otherwise restricted and redefined. Oversight in the selection and behavior of gurus was also introduced.[88]

The most significant changes were those that affected the traditional stature of the guru. The GBC created a new category that was designated as "initiating master." No longer would gurus, appointed after the reform, engage in "conflict of interest" as had the *guru ācāryas*.[89] The new gurus were to be full-fledged initiating masters (*dīkṣā gurus*), albeit without public devotee worship; nor would they be allowed to exercise exclusive power, whether religious or secular, in their "apostolate." The GBC would constitute the "official" authority that would oversee the masters, and the latter were to submit to the prescribed discipline.[90]

In the earlier system, *zonal ācāryas* rarely allowed other gurus to preach in their regions unless the event was structured in such a way that the visitor was clearly subordinate to the *ācārya*. Under the jurisdiction of one or more GBC members, a guru could now move freely about and preach. In turn, gurus would not be required to demonstrate personal charisma; they were mediators of the absolute, unique charismatic authority of the *founder ācārya*, Bhaktivedānta. Their new mission would be to operate within the confines of collegiality. This change from the former system and the traditional concept of a guru was revolutionary.[91] Although there would be deviations from what could be called the purely institutional interests of ISKCON, the new system was an improvement. As Larry D. Shinn has noted: "[T]he impressive fact for any careful observer of ISKCON's history is that it has been able to evolve in a very short time from a charismatic movement to a relatively stable institution in the face of a hostile external environment and a volatile governance structure within."[92] Indeed, when the 1987 meetings ended, the GBC had endorsed practically every reform proposal submitted.

## THE THIRD PHASE

### From Institutional Commitment to Individual Responsibility

For those who shared the reformers' vision, the late 1980s was a time of renaissance, but for others, the changes created commotion and bewilderment. ISKCON had spread well beyond the temples and communities, and it was moving toward an era of greater personal responsibility, which implied a major adjustment for thousands of adherents.

The motivational vacuum created by the desertions was partly filled by a providential generational change with a new class of novices. Still, in the areas formerly assigned to the departed gurus, the number of defections was high.[93] People had lost their anchors, and it was not easy to re-instill faith in such members. In the U.S. the decrease in full-time adherents and communities was dramatic.[94] At the same time, the number of Kṛṣṇa centers in Europe doubled and the number of full-time European members increased significantly from 1987 to 1994.[95] A similar trend was registered in India and Latin America.

There was a setback in 1987 when the New Vṛndāvana case exploded into the media. The West Virginia community, led by Kīrtanānda Svāmī, had divorced itself from ISKCON in the summer of 1985 and was expelled in 1987. The adherents remained faithful to their guru, and ISKCON lost a large estate and its considerable population. For years, New Vṛndāvana had been under scrutiny from all sides—from the media and local law enforcement, for instance—and when police investigating a missing person case uncovered clues that led to the temple compound, the FBI was summoned to conduct a search. The federal officers found the remains of devotee Charles St. Denis (1948- 1983), who had mysteriously disappeared in 1983. They also confiscated a large quantity of merchandise that bore evidence of copyright infringements. Again, the GBC invited New Vṛndāvana residents to rejoin ISKCON without Kīrtanānda Svāmī, but the besieged community fell into a defensive position and resisted the offer.[96] In the wake of these events, a polemical account of the community's troubles, *Monkey on a Stick,* damaged not only the public image of New Vṛndāvana but of ISKCON as well.[97]

Still, the GBC pushed ahead with its reform program, endorsing the principle that "all can become gurus."[98] The number of authorized spiritual masters increased from thirty to sixty in 1990 and to eighty in 1993.[99] Not everyone was pleased. At the one extreme, some adherents wanted more radical change. The *ṛtvik* controversy reappeared and spread discord with regard to ISKCON's official policy, saying that officiating masters held proxy authority only, as representatives of the one true guru, Bhaktivedānta Svāmī.[100]

## TRENDS AND CHANGES IN THE 1990S

Oblivious to such controversies, new converts were being won to ISKCON in eastern Europe in impressive numbers. The doors to the former Soviet Union were opened in 1990 as never before due to the dramatic political changes of 1989. Missionaries made entries into Bulgaria, Czechoslovakia, Hungary, Poland, Romania, and the former Yugoslavia, and by the end of the year, the former Soviet Union hosted about a hundred ISKCON centers populated by five hundred residents and backed by almost 10,000 sympathizers.[101] As ISKCON launched intense and dynamic activities on this new frontier, by the end of 1990, the North European Bhaktivedānta Book Trust had published over a million copies of the founder's books in Russian, all distributed in less than a year.

American ISKCON musicians toured eastern Europe in 1991 to an unprecedented response. Young people found themselves drawn to the ambiance of the open-air concerts where these American "apostles" preached an interesting new "gospel," and a crescendo of conversions followed.

After the new subway opened in Moscow, nearly all of the 3,500 subway cars boasted advertisements of Bhaktivedānta's books, including an invitation to discover the ancient traditions of India. The five million daily subway passengers responded well to the striking, innovative posters that showed little trace of U.S. commercialism, and the campaign generated book sales in the hundreds of thousands.

Eastern Europe welcomed the unconventional nature of ISKCON's pioneers at the same time that, in the United States, the religion was going through an altogether different evolution. Leaders were worried about the diminishing revenues and beginning to think about new ways of financing their operations. During the July 1991 celebration of the twenty-fifth year of the movement's founding, the ISKCON Foundation took birth and generated new income to sustain and strengthen the movement. The foundation directed its attention beyond the devotee population to areas of the United States that had high concentrations of immigrant Hindus. This demographic proved to be increasingly receptive to and acquainted with ISKCON.[102] In the meantime, the movement kept growing in eastern Europe, particularly in the former Soviet Union where the expansion seemed unstoppable.[103]

A reason to celebrate presented itself as the centennial of Bhaktivedānta's birth approached. Already in 1992, so-called "family reunions" were introduced first in Los Angeles in May and then in Melbourne in June. The reunions brought all of Bhaktivedānta's direct disciples together, as well as followers of the new gurus, all of whom wanted to commemorate the figure and the teachings of the founder. The celebrations were repeated elsewhere with increasing frequency. The rationale was to reinforce relationships among members and look for new forms of dialogue. It was also hoped that the gatherings would help heal ruptures and misunderstandings that had occurred within the movement.

In the same spirit, alumni of ISKCON schools met in Los Angeles. This inspired a board of GBC members to commission a survey of second-generation ISKCON members, the results of which were troubling: many boys and girls who were brought up in ISKCON boarding schools (*aśrama-gurukula*), suffered from an identity crisis and social integration problems.[104] When the schools were closed in the 1980s due to the period of declining revenues, the transition was traumatic for the students. Concern over this issue influenced much of the future direction and aspirations of the movement. Indeed, it would draw increasing attention both from within and without as members found the status of their children to be deeply disturbing and as activists and reporters followed in tow. Many believe that much more needs to be done, that as yet, far too little attention has been paid the issue.

Missionaries in the receptive eastern European countries experienced significant difficulties for the first time in 1993 as their successes were beginning to catch the attention of government and religious authorities. A government board in Hungary found ISKCON to be a "destructive cult" and recommended that it be banned. ISKCON Communication Europe[105] mobilized and was able to draw international attention to their plight. Eventually ISKCON was granted official government recognition in Hungary.

In Armenia, authorities raised similar objections the next year in what became a recurring theme of official suspicion and prejudice among the general population. In 1995 the anxiety over ISKCON escalated into violent attacks in Yerevan, Armenia; Sukhumi, Georgia; and Rostov, Russia. Unaccustomed to the degree of religious pluralism enjoyed in western Europe, the eastern bloc struggled as it worked to accommodate 5,500 religious organizations registered in the former Soviet Union by 1991 and a full 11,500 by 1996.

Another decisive change occurred within the movement among lay, non-cloistered believers whose role was increasingly acknowledged as being legitimate and important. Married members had not always been warmly received within the rigid institutional structure and had been driven to relocate themselves away from the temple, both spatially and culturally. By this time, ISKCON had lost the impetus to create a utopian society, and many individuals and families were increasingly finding themselves drifting into lifestyles that were more in keeping with the external world. In the process, their sense of alienation contributed to the impoverishment of the movement.

There have been at least two types of lay people. The first is a former full-time resident who has moved away from the temple or community to raise a family but still associates with the institution. The second is a sympathizer who is not allowed or does not desire to reside within an ISKCON community but adheres to a novice practice at home. The profiles vary according to an individual's spiritual and practical considerations. Yet, the advent of the nuclear family within ISKCON society presaged the end of communitarianism and became the most influential development in the thirty-year history of the religion's social life. The number of families eventually outnumbered the number of celibates living communally and reached a ratio of 70:30 in America. The reality of the situation implied the need for a different strategy of recruitment and self-sustenance and managerial models.

At this point, ISKCON could no longer rely solely on its internal members. Leaders had come to realize that lay people who lived beyond the confines of the temple were a vital resource, and they began devoting increasing attention to the accommodation of these congregational members. The change in emphasis produced obvious advantages from the beginning. On March 16, 1994, in London, ISKCON organized a protest against the closure of the Bhaktivedānta Manor Temple, an elegant suburban structure that had come to attract Hindus from all over the London area. The protest march drew 36,000 participants, most of them Indian immigrants who were accustomed to attending religious ceremonies and festivities at the manor and considered its closure as a serious breach of religious freedom.[106] The coordinated outreach to lay people outside the temple, offering recreational and spiritual programs for members and sympathizers alike, allowed ISKCON to be considered part of the greater community, thus favoring the legitimization and maintenance of the movement's core.

This model was fruitful in Great Britain, so it was implemented elsewhere, partly to repopulate the communities that otherwise had seemed doomed to extinction. In the early 1990s, the Hare Kṛṣṇa community of Alachua, Florida, began encouraging families to settle in the area surrounding the temple. The families were thus able to take advantage of daily religious functions and contribute to the temple's expenses while otherwise living independent lives. As of 2001, the Alachua neighborhood was inhabited by about four hundred individuals, all tied to ISKCON in various ways.

## ONE HUNDRED YEARS AFTER THE FOUNDER'S BIRTH

The centennial of Bhaktivedānta's birth was celebrated all over the world with religious and cultural events. A March of One Hundred Countries was held in the founder's native city of Calcutta in the spring of 1996. Devotees from around the world—one hundred countries—provided a visible demonstration of their founder's international success. Two days later, the march moved to Delhi to witness the inauguration of a large new ISKCON temple and was attended by such dignitaries as the Indian prime minister. Other centennial temples were inaugurated in western India's Ahmedabad, once home to Mohandas Gandhi, and the southern city of Bangalore. That same year, ISKCON produced a television documentary series entitled "Abhay Caran" for broadcast on the Indian National Network.

Thirty years after ISKCON's founding, leaders saw in this additional benchmark opportunities both to celebrate and to evaluate the movement's successes and failures, especially through the recurrent Family Reunions. The prevailing mood in 1996 was expressed by an ISKCON official at a conference on social development held that year:

> Over the last twenty-five years the social image that ISKCON has had of itself has remained basically the same, whereas its actual identity has changed radically. Now ISKCON is debating the issues arising from this gap between its image and its actual identity. Introspection, redefinition, and reorganization are the orders of the day. In short, ISKCON has embarked on institutional self-realization. Although not everyone in ISKCON will welcome the prospect of reassessing and possibly changing how our society works, many devotees feel it is an urgent need. Some devotees have expressed their dissatisfaction by leaving ISKCON. Nowadays, self-analysis and re-evaluation are normal procedures on all levels of ISKCON's organization. Negative reactions to social progress in ISKCON are viewed as another valuable contribution to a debate, rather than as threats to development or as restrictions.[107]

The year 1996 saw two important ISKCON conferences on social development, one in India and one in Florida, and proposals that would characterize the future ISKCON attitude toward the "things of this world."

Although most of the centennial celebrations took place in India,[108] there were reverberations as far away as Poland where thousands of people attended Kṛṣṇa festivals that summer. Even so, storm clouds gathered during this auspicious year and threatened to eclipse whatever progress was achieved through public relations. In 1996 and 1997, two more gurus stepped down from their positions, reviving old controversies as they expressed their discontent in letters of resignation.[109] In the aftermath of these desertions, with similar defections over the next few years, a new polemic emerged.[110] Detractors claimed that the masters authorized by the GBC were not qualified to ensure a stable system of succession, although these critics could not agree among themselves on a suitable counter-measure. Some favored the *ṛtvik-vāda* view that religious authority was vested in the founder alone with gurus acting as his proxies. Others hoped for the "messianic" rise of a master whose "self-effulgent" character would undisputedly lead the movement forward in unity.[111]

For its part, the GBC hardened its stance, emphasizing the central position of Bhaktivedānta Svāmī as the primary source of spiritual authority. But the GBC also wanted to legitimize the *dīkṣā* gurus, or initiating masters, as long as they mirrored the words and will of the founder.[112] It could not have been otherwise since Bhaktivedānta was the only undisputed stronghold of integrity, charisma, and spiritual depth.[113] All these different factions tried to legitimize their particular views by appealing to the founder's authority.

The dilemma may be seen as one that hung on two horns

of the same steer—the institutionalization of charisma and the vitality of the institutions. Regulations may be symptomatic of a compromise with the outside world and a disproportionate degree of secularization. To put it in Mark Chaves's words, "[D]ecline of religious authorities thus determines secularization."[114]

This problem is not peculiar to ISKCON. In fact, every institution struggles with the management of charisma. It is a difficult issue. It is nevertheless the foundation of both the practical and symbolic health of an organization. The topic was raised by sociologist Max Weber, who wrote that charisma is "a quality regarded as extraordinary ... pertaining to a personality [who] is considered as [being endowed] with powers and properties supernatural or superhuman, or at least specifically exceptional, not accessible to others, or as sent by God, or draped with an exemplary value."[115]

The issue is central to institutions like ISKCON that have relied on the extraordinary gifts of a single individual in their formative years. Religions, along with corporations and other organizations, try to preserve the charisma of their founders, or to guarantee its Weberian "routinization," with little success. Regulations and canonization contribute to the stifling of enthusiasm, which is the very dynamism and elasticity that powered the group in the first place. The result is crystallization, bureaucracy, and stratification.

According to Ernst Troeltsch's terminology, this is how a sect transforms itself into a church. It leaves the egalitarian and ascetic spirit of the founders behind.[116] When the sect begins exerting wider influence, when it attempts to "dominate the world" rather than to "refute it," it becomes a church. ISKCON faced this risk when it attempted to renovate itself without betraying its roots. It should be remembered that "to succeed, a new religious movement must not make its peace with this world too rapidly or too fully. A faith too accommodated to worldliness lacks power for continued conversion."[117]

## IMPACT ON ACTUAL LIVES
### From Political to Socio-Economic History

The developments within the movement changed the daily social lives of residents of ISKCON communities and temples and non-resident believers alike. A significant number of devotees left the temples and lost their proselytizing zeal after the founder's death. A likely cause for the desertions was the lack of institutional and cultural cohesion from the leadership at the time.[118]

The shift away from monastic membership engendered problems of identity, social connectedness, and questions about what responsibility the movement had to its new, extended family.[119] About 75 percent of the membership today adheres to ISKCON principles from an external lay position.

This occurred on a similar track but on a delayed schedule around the world. As the movement waned in the U.S., it was just coming into full bloom in Europe;[120] but the succession of events repeated themselves in Europe about ten years later—something to keep in mind in considering the dynamics of ISKCON community building and social development.

Wherever ISKCON settled, it began with the same strategy for financing its basic needs through the distribution and sale of Bhaktivedānta's literature. This was known as *sāṃkīrtana,*[121] the Indian term that, among Caitanya's followers, implied traditional spiritual practices.[122] Bhaktivedānta used the term to imply that doctrine could be disseminated in a way that was grounded in theology and practicality.[123] Broadcasting this faith abroad should be self-sustaining, in Bhaktivedānta's view, which is why the Hare Kṛṣṇas have always stressed book sales.[124]

The book distribution began in the late 1960s through a strategy that involved personal, one-on-one contact. Originally, the proselytizing was performed in lay dress, but the classic Indian robes were soon preferred in some countries because it drew more attention and yielded better results. Christmastime yielded the best conditions for selling and fund raising. Even today, most ISKCON members help with the so-called "Christmas marathon."[125] As the first devotees devised methods for winning over typical urban indifference, they found that if they danced and chanted *mantras*, this created an exotic religious atmosphere that attracted onlookers and prompted inquiries. Even so, direct sales pitches were still the most efficient means of propagation.

Sales followed a predictable pattern. They increased gradually to a certain point and thereafter steadily declined. Sales grew in the United States until 1976 and remained stable in 1977, then waned until, by the 1980s, they were less than a fourth of what they had been in 1976. It became necessary to import and sell Indian incense, paintings, and carpets to subsidize the decline. Until the mid-1980s, most ISKCON centers were maintained solely by book distribution, so the reduced sales meant that much of what members had come to expect in the way of activities and community amenities had to be abandoned. As one scholar wrote: "All this explains why, in the life of Hare Kṛṣṇa communities, it was so important to economize individual energies to a maximum extent."[126]

Plunging revenues coincided with the internal crisis at the demise of the founder. Because "non-productive" families proved to be a drain on resources, they were dismissed from the communities. This created a vicious cycle, compounded by dwindling community enthusiasm, vanishing funds, fewer members, institutional bewilderment, and near-sighted and impulsive remedies.[127]

An unplanned decentralization took place because the structure that had supported the authority figures had collapsed. Coincidentally, the criteria for judging whether someone was a valid member changed at this time at the community level. No longer would one's value depend solely on deeds performed within the temple or on one's availability for community projects. The passage from homogeneity to self-determination became a viable option, and where someone chose to live was less important than the spiritual values one held. Paradoxically, new recruits were now being advised to avoid joining a community and to remain within their existing social circumstances until better times.[128]

The institutional innovations breathed new life into fund raising, but some of the strategies, including "picking," or panhandling, added to the deterioration of the movement's image.[129] From the end of the 1970s to the early 1980s—after the Jonestown massacre—the public became even more wary of new religions.[130] Anti-cult exponents who had seemed bent on ridding the world of diversity found renewed energy in the wake of the so-called sect scare.[131]

When ISKCON experienced its revival in Europe in the early 1980s, the number of European centers exploded to forty-three by the end of 1983, where there had been only eleven in 1975. A second boom occurred in the early 1990s and brought the total to one hundred centers across Europe by 1994. However, the conversion rate was more modest than the percentage increase in centers.

No doubt, the political transformation of 1989 played a major role in ISKCON's second European expansion. This is shown by the fact that from 1989 to 1994, thirty-four Hare Kṛṣṇa structures were built in eastern Europe. The increase in book distribution recorded at the time is also attributable to the expanded market rather than to a resurgence of interest among western Europeans.

Another reason that ISKCON centers were multiplying throughout Europe is that the model for ISKCON communities had changed. Europeans were building small preaching centers around which a community of non-resident believers could gravitate. Maintenance costs were thus abated and the geographic distribution was increased.

There were management failures and defections in the mid-1990s at the large ISKCON centers in England, France, Italy, and Spain which caused a change of heart in recruitment strategies. Between 1996 and 1999, the socio-economic profile of ISKCON was tested, and the shock-wave from the desertion of northern Europe's zonal guru resulted in a new-found interest in change. Until then, progress was achieved according to what had been a perfectly workable, even exemplary model of development.

# 2.

# Practices and Rituals

## THE ATTIRE

The distinctive dress that Hare Kṛṣṇa devotees came to be known for is not unusual in India. But, in fact, the classic figure of the dancing, chanting devotee with a shaved head and saffron robe—the icon of religious sects in the West—has now nearly disappeared. Today, most ISKCON members are laics and reside outside of the temple compounds, wear standard dress, and avoid anything that would identify them as Hare Kṛṣṇas at work or elsewhere in public.

Full-time members do continue to wear traditional Indian robes, and among the residents of the temples and communities, men still shave their heads, leaving a tuft of hair (*śikhā*) to fall onto the nape of the neck. The men's robe, the *dhotī*, is white to indicate a married man and saffron for celibates and senior members who have taken the vow of renunciation. Women who reside in the communities wear long, multicolored lengths of cloth, *sāṛīs*, that are wrapped around the whole body and sometimes over the top of the head. Their hair is usually kept long but tidily braided.

Full-time members apply the traditional marks (*tilaka*) of the Gauḍīya Vaiṣṇava tradition to their forehead, arms, chest, and abdomen once a day using clay that comes from sacred Indian rivers and lakes. They also wear a beaded necklace that is made out of *tulasī* wood; *tulasī* is a sacred plant that is worshiped by Vaiṣṇavas.

In considering a devotee's daily practices, one should keep in mind that there are two distinct dimensions of belonging as either an "internal resident devotee" or an "external devotee." Since the percentage of lay members is much higher than the percentage of temple residents, it would be wrong to overlook the lay practices. However, the daily observances of non-resident believers derive, to some extent, from the temple liturgy.

ISKCON claims to be a modern expression of the older Gauḍīya Vaiṣṇava tradition.[1] However, it is important to remember that its ritual and liturgical practices were adapted according to its founder's vision and its international dimension. In some ways, it diverges from other religious communities in Bengal, Orissa, and Uttar Pradesh which claim a similar heritage.[2] This is not surprising since in the Hindu experience one would expect variations on a tradition[3] as influenced by geography, historical-political context, social dimensions, language, and the figure of the leader.

## THE IDEAL DAILY PRACTICES AND THEIR APPLICATIONS WITHIN THE LAITY

The following is meant to be a description of ISKCON practices[4] as they agree with and diverge from other Vaiṣṇava realities. Whereas the emphasis within ISKCON is on certain liturgical and doctrinal elements, they constitute one possible interpretation of Gauḍīya principles, and it is the combination of these elements that comprises ISKCON orthodoxy.[5]

Conforming to common Hindu habits, ISKCON devotees

begin each day very early, about two hours before dawn, with a meticulous body cleansing, which is considered to be a necessary prerequisite for ritual activities. Then comes the body "spiritualization" when the traditional symbols such as the *tilaka* are applied to the body. Following these individual preparations, devotees meet in the temple room for the *mangala-ārati* ceremony at 4:30 A.M. This ritual is widely observed in South Asia with slight variations. It involves ritualistically awakening and greeting the temple deities[6] and singing hymns in Sanskrit (*kīrtana, bhajana*) for their pleasure, accompanied by traditional instruments such as the two-faced drum and brass cymbals.

The deities are the focal point around which all daily activities in the temple revolve. The statues are worshiped as if they were living beings. For instance, all food is ritually offered to the deities before it is consumed by the devotees as consecrated *prasāda*. There are variations in the worship rituals, which may be simple or quite elaborate according to the available facilities and human resources. What is common to all temples is that the devotees ritually bathe the deities in the morning, clothe them in full vestments one or two times every day, and make food offerings to them at different hours of the day.

The wakening ritual ends at about 5:15 A.M., and the next two hours are allotted for individual meditation with the help of a rosary crafted out of sacred wood (*akṣa-mālā*) on which *mantras* are counted. Devotees are expected to chant or murmur (*jāpa*)[7] the names of Kṛṣṇa[8] with complete concentration in an atmosphere of praise and invocation to god. In ISKCON, this practice is a fundamental part of all religious and missionary activities.[9]

After meditation, the collective ceremony known as *śṛṅgāra-ārati* begins at 7:15 A.M., allowing devotees to admire the new costumes the *mūrtis* are dressed in. The costumes are elaborate and are changed every day. Thereafter comes *guru-pūjā*, the daily worship of the founder, Bhaktivedānta.

Around 8:00 A.M., after some additional prayers and songs, the residents gather in the temple room to hear a lecture by a senior member of the community or a traveling master. The topic usually comes from the *Bhāgavata-purāṇa*, which is the central scripture in ISKCON and was the founder's favorite. Bhaktivedānta not only translated the *Bhāgavata-purāṇa* into English, he also provided followers with his own extensive, published commentary on it.[10] The liturgical session is usually over by 9:00 A.M. when it is time for the customary vegetarian breakfast in the refectory.

Thereafter, each devotee performs various practical duties assigned to him or her according to the circumstances, needs, and scope of the community. Members might engage in book production and sales, cooking, gardening, priestly or liturgical duties, or office work.

Around 2:00 P.M., the members reconvene for lunch, followed by an hour or two of privacy when devotees rest or read religious literature. Work is then resumed and continues until 7:00 P.M. At that time, devotees gather in the temple room to sing hymns (*sandhyā-ārati*), sometimes followed by a brief lecture on the *Bhagavad-gītā*, which was dear to Bhaktivedānta.[11] Finally at 8:00 P.M., the *śayana-ārati* is the final ceremony wherein the deities are invited to rest for the night. There is an optional light supper of milk, cereal, and fruit; then the devotees retire to their rooms, sometimes to read scriptural passages before sleeping.

External devotees generally observe the same schedule, although more or less rigidly according to the piety and conscientiousness of each person. There are non-initiated devotees who follow the canonical schedul there are senior initiates who are more la keep aloof from the community. Wheth eran, many of the external devotees admire the tem style, and in some cases they express nostalgia or seem to suffer from an inferiority complex with regard to the lifestyle of full-time residents. However, it is important to note that the laic congregation's growth—its expansion beyond the controlled communities—produced new forms of participation and belonging, and hence, orthodoxy became more moderate and accommodating of the laic dimension.[12]

## INITIATION RITES, VOWS, AND SACRAMENTS

The complex and varied nature of ISKCON rituals excludes a thorough examination here, although a few milestones along the believer's path deserve special mention. To begin with, the novitiate usually lasts at least six months. During this time, a candidate is encouraged to choose which authorized guru he or she will follow as a disciple.[13] This is the first step toward the "first initiation," or *harināma-dīkṣā*, when the adept is told the holy names of Hari and takes his or her vows.[14]

After a period of verification and confirmation, the novice completes a questionnaire with thirteen doctrinal and institutional questions. He must then receive the blessings of the local temple authorities, who attest to the genuineness of the novice's character and motivations. The individual is then fit to be initiated. A fire sacrifice is performed. During the ceremony, the novice solemnly takes his vows before his guru, who changes his name to a Sanskrit designation. This new name links the believer to a particular aspect or form of god. The name always includes the suffix *dāsa* for men and *dāsī* for women, in both cases signifying a servant." It reminds the believer of his state of servitude before god and guru. Thereafter, the devotee is known in the community as, for instance, Kṛṣṇadāsa or Kṛṣṇadāsī.

During the initiation ceremony, the candidate promises to abide by certain ethical standards, including both positive prescriptions and negative prohibitions. The founder emphasized four "regulative principles": "No illicit sex life, no meat-eating, no intoxication, no gambling."[15] The candidate promises to chant a precise number of *mantras* every day, along with other duties.[16]

A year or more later, a devotee can be considered eligible for a "second initiation," a further rite that enables him to perform specific liturgical procedures. On this occasion, the initiate receives the status of a *brāhmaṇa*,[17] symbolized by the sacred thread (*yajñopavīta*),[18] which is held when chanting the *gāyatrī-mantra*.[19] This ceremony was first introduced by Bhaktivedānta Svāmī's guru, Bhaktisiddhānta Sarasvatī, who had distanced himself from the traditionalists by rejecting the idea that only those who were *brāhmaṇas* by birth (*jāti*) could perform sacrificial rites or other activities linked to the brahmanical status.[20]

Other important rites of passage in a Kṛṣṇa life include the marriage ceremony (*vivāha-yajña*) and, at a mature age, initiation into the order of renunciation (*saṇnyāsa*). In its historic evolution, ISKCON has drawn from various Vaiṣṇava traditions to establish its own liturgy for various events. Where the founder chose not to establish a fixed liturgy, ISKCON leaders have filled in the gaps, deriving notions from external authorities, to create a cultural setting that included all the normal "rites of passage."[21]

# 3.

# Doctrine and Theology

The preaching of Caitanya (1486-1533) and his followers produced several Vaiṣṇava trajectories that flourished mainly in northern India. They were collectively known as the Gauḍīya school because of their Bengali origin[1] and in order to distinguish them from other Vaiṣṇava traditions.[2] Gauḍīya Vaiṣṇavism[3] was inherited by ISKCON through a complex and somewhat tentative historical link. Initially, the mediators in this transmission were Ṭhākura Bhaktivinoda (1838-1914)[4] and his son Bhaktisiddhānta Sarasvatī (1874-1937),[5] both of whom actualized and revised several Gauḍīya doctrinal tenets. The latter was a particularly courageous reformer who modernized the tradition. In doing so, he followed in the footsteps of his father, a progressive preacher who, in his day, circulated in Bengali intellectual circles where an integration of Indian culture with Western scientific language and cultural strategies was promoted.[6] This legacy of activism and doctrinal refinement continued in the life and works of Bhaktivedānta Svāmī as he adapted ISKON's Gauḍīya teachings to an international dimension. ISKCON can be seen as an attempt to represent the composite Gauḍīya Vaiṣṇava universe[7] to a modern audience, and to that extent, it differs from more conservative Gauḍīya communities.[8] However, as variations are common in South Asian culture and religion, this is seen as part of a natural and unavoidable phenomenon.[9]

## A BRIEF HISTORY OF THE GAUḌĪYA LINE

The Gauḍīya tradition is understood to be a direct development and revitalization of the *kṛṣṇa-bhakti* (devotion to Kṛṣṇa) movement, albeit with unique characteristics.[10] It began when Viśvaṃbhara, also called Nimāi Paṇḍita and Gaurāṅga, was born in Navadvīpa, Bengal, in February 1486.[11] After his *saṇnyāsa* initiation, he became better known as Kṛṣṇa Caitanya and a central figure in the *bhakti* movement. Indeed, among his followers, he was considered to be god himself, descended to earth.[12]

Because his acts and teachings were mostly devotional, it is not always easy to isolate a consistent trend in his doctrines.[13] However, it was the vitality of his preaching and the renaissance it generated that explain his stature: "Although Caitanya was not the founder of the Vaiṣṇava movement in Bengal, he was its revivalist. Evidence that the movement existed well before his time is ample, as has been suggested. The lyrics of such poets as Caṇḍīdāsa and Vidyāpati ... were 'read with pleasure' by Caitanya."[14]

Most Gauḍīya branches maintain that Caitanya's cardinal points were passed down through the writings of his followers, where no more than eight brief stanzas can be directly attributed to Caitanya.[15] Because Caitanya chose not to enunciate his doctrine in writing, his contemporaries systematized what they remembered of his views, principally the chroniclers Rūpa and Sanātana; their nephew Jīva, whose *Ṣaṭ-sandarbha* is considered the best compendium of Gauḍīya theology;[16] and later Baladeva Vidyābhūṣana, who wrote a commentary on the *Brahma-sūtra* at the beginning of the eighteenth century.

In other words, while it is impossible to ascertain the exact nature of Caitanya's teachings, scholars and believers alike turn to his immediate followers' hagiographic works that report dialogues and episodes of his life.[17] The biography, *Caitanya-caritāmṛta*, written in Bengali by Kṛṣṇadāsa Kavirāja, also known as Kavirāja Gosvāmī, has come to be viewed as canonical. Kavirāja was not a direct contemporary of Caitanya, but he knew many of the guru's intimate followers. The work is a thinly disguised theological treatise that borrows key points from the works of the so-called *gosvāmīs* who lived with Caitanya and received personal instructions from him. The *gosvāmīs* achieved the monumental task of compiling all of the textual material that is available today in the fields of early Gauḍīya theology, poetry, liturgy, and hymnology.[18] Among these respected men, "Rūpa Gosvāmī was the prime exponent of a blend of aesthetics and psychology that provided a theoretical framework for Caitanya's emotional *bhakti* and influenced other subsequent *saṃpradāyas*," or sects, "including those of Nimbārka and Vallabha."[19]

However difficult a universally acceptable description of Caitanya's thought is, his influence on the society and culture is indisputable, both in terms of religious practices and art. His vicarious contribution to literature was especially significant: "Rūpa Gosvāmī, along with his brother Sanātan and his nephew Jīva, [was] the greatest representative of the Brindaban school of Vaishnavism, [who] deeply influenced the post-Caitanya Bengali *padas* [poetic mantras] by his Sanskrit book on poetics entitled *Ujjvalanīlamaṇi*. With a typically Indian sense for system and classification, he categorized, divided and subdivided the 'subject-matters' of the *padas* and laid down rules of how the devotion to Krishna should be expressed. ... In Caitanya's time there started a mighty heyday of *pada* literature, both in Bengali and in Brajabuli."[20]

## THEORETICAL PROFILE OF GAUḌĪYA VAIṢṆAVA THOUGHT

As already mentioned, some crucial theological issues have been diversely interpreted by the various currents of Gauḍīya Vaiṣṇava. Nevertheless, the branches that took root in the West—including ISKCON and most of the other Gauḍīya institutions deriving from Bhaktivedānta's guru and his guru's father—largely agree on basic tenets. Out of practical considerations, this discussion will be confined to these areas of agreement, especially as they relate to ISKCON, with only a few comments on some key points of divergence.[21] The central issues, about which a considerable amount of theoretical elaboration has been assembled, are the link between disciple and master (*guru-śiṣya-sambandha*), chanting the holy names (*hari-nāma-saṃkīrtana*), the daily service offered to Kṛṣṇa's image (*mūrti-sevā*), hearing the scriptural passages that deal with Kṛṣṇa's teachings and his pastimes with Rādhā, his consort (*nāma-guṇa-līlā-smaraṇa*), and service to Kṛṣṇa's devotees, regardless of their rank and social status (*bhakta-sevā*). Another noteworthy feature is the emphasis on devotion to the divine couple, Rādhā-Kṛṣṇa; all of the believer's daily activities are to be devoted only to them.

To gain a better insight into Gauḍīya theology, it is useful to start with a more familiar and universal issue such as the nature of god and his relationship with human beings. All Gauḍīya believers consider Kṛṣṇa to be the supreme divinity.[22] He is conceived as being a dynamic synthesis of immanence and transcendence. His deeds are therefore eternal pastimes (*nitya-līlā*) and belong to a superior order of existence, even while they are visible on earth. Kṛṣṇa is endowed with potencies (*śakti*), which are subdivided into three general categories: internal, external, and marginal.[23] These energies are respectively considered to be god's self-contained potency, his illusory potency in the visible world, and his manifestation through individual entities, or particles, which exist throughout his creation. Through these energies, god pervades whatever exists; still, he is not necessarily present everywhere, as said in the *Bhagavad-gītā*: "All this world is strung on me in the form of the Unmanifest; all creatures exist in me, but I do not exist in them. And again, the creatures do not exist in me—behold my supernal yoga! While sustaining the creatures and giving them being, my self does not exist in them. Just as the vast wind which goes everywhere is yet always contained within space, so, realize this, all creatures are contained in me."[24]

The same character of simultaneous unity and difference (*bheda-abheda*) marks the relation (*sambandha*) between individuals and god. Through devotion, the soul can unveil its role in the pastimes (*līlā*) that are eternally enacted in the spiritual realm (*vaikuṇṭha*); this requires a purification from material inhibitions (*anartha*), and the process can take more than one existence. Of course, this implies belief in the cycle of rebirth (*saṃsāra*). The soul's role is to conform to its deepest inclination and allow itself to form an exclusive relationship with god.

The creation has a preparatory and evocative role: in it, the spirit can endeavor to propel itself toward Kṛṣṇa's heaven (*goloka-vṛndāvana*). The world is a transformation of god's energy (*śakti-pariṇāma*), and it is thus real, although temporary, and not false or illusory.[25] Devotion to god (*kṛṣṇa-bhakti*) is ontologically inherent in each and every individual being,[26] and everyone can revive his or her relationship with divinity only through the cultivation of this devotion, never through other paths such as speculative or ritualistic means. One can only overcome worldly ties through the strength of devotional love.

A true devotee does not demand anything from Kṛṣṇa; he is, rather, content with his love for him, deriving an infinite happiness from the satisfaction of his beloved god.[27] Love for god is itself a divine manifestation, god's own pleasure potency (*hlādinī-śakti*), and is the founding reality of human experience: a soul's love for god can either be confined to a sleeping state or revived to a waking state whenever favorable circumstances occur through association with and inspiration from a guru.

There are formative paths that can be followed to evoke such devotion. These are first of all to be taught by a guru, who transmits god's devotional energy (*bhakti*) to a qualified individual. As we have seen, the characteristics of the guru are a matter of much debate within ISKCON. Nonetheless, there are certain traits that have been traditionally attributed to this figure. His basic task is to educate disciples in spiritual practices, to introduce them to doctrine, and to dispel contextual misunderstandings with sound explanations. The disciple's duty is to tie himself exclusively to Kṛṣṇa with all of the faculties at his disposal.[28]

These shared doctrinal features conform broadly to ISKCON's theology, but there are other points of doctrine about which various Gauḍīya traditions disagree.[29] Caitanya's preaching produced many branches, and while they share a common root, they tend to favor divergent hermeneutical approaches to the canon and thereby incompatible opinions on some issues. An example would be the status of *bhakti* within each individual soul. In ISKCON, *bhakti* is regarded as "inborn" or "rooted" in each person. Outside of ISKCON's theological framework, this is not a unanimously accepted view. Some Gauḍīya theologians maintain that *bhakti* is mysteriously bestowed by god at the time of one's spiritual awakening and that it is therefore not "inborn." Others believe that *bhakti* is neither "innate" nor ontologically "given"; it is instead "donated" or "transmitted" anew by a guru who, when moved by divine compassion, sows *bhakti* seeds in a candidate's heart.[30]

These subtle doctrinal differences have rather weighty consequences. As seen throughout history, a slight difference in interpretation or outlook can lead to quite dissonant *Weltanschauungen.* In this case, the choice regarding the status of *bhakti* produces an altogether different understanding of the guru's role, which in turn implies unique sets of rules. Moreover, if all beings are equally predisposed to achieve and develop *kṛṣṇa-bhakti,* not just subjected to god's unfathomable choice, there are noteworthy implications in the issue of theodicy or, more broadly, in the problem of the existence of evil. The matter is also linked to the "retribution of actions" (*karman*) and to the idea of predestination.[31]

For Gauḍīya traditions closer to ISKCON, the deep-rootedness of *bhakti* in the individual represents a central tenet with implications for their "missionology": belief in a devotional predisposition, ontologically inherent within each individual, leads to the expectation of an "awakening" through the "cultivation" of this "innate" attitude. Public chanting of holy names (*nagara-saṃkīrtana*), which was so dear to ISKCON's founder, can be understood from this perspective. By hearing god's names, the individual may take his first steps toward the natural awakening of devotion to god.[32] A statement often used to support this concept is derived from the *śikṣāṣṭakas,* the only direct teachings of Caitanya: "Hari is to be celebrated."[33] From this perspective, the progressive stages of *bhakti* are interpreted as a gradual "awakening," and the believer is eventually expected to pass from a regulated devotional practice (*vaidhi-bhakti*) to a spontaneous attraction to god (*rāgānugā-bhakti*): "These are the different states of the appearance of *preman:* first *śraddhā,* i.e. faith, next *sādhu-saṅga* or association with saints, after that *bhajana-kriyā* or spiritual practices, next to it is *anartha-nivṛtti,* i.e. cessation of all offenses or obstacles, next to it is *niṣṭhā* or firmness, which is followed by *ruci* or taste, next is *āsakti* or attachment, after this is *bhāva* [attitude], and then appears *preman.* These are the different stages of the appearance of *preman* in the heart of a person who undergoes spiritual practices."[34] Devotion to god is expected to become so intense that a mature devotee no longer aspires to a state of liberation (*mokṣa*) from the perennial cycle of rebirth; he is utterly content as long as he can serve his beloved divinity, life after life. Caitanya described this state of mind in his *śikṣāṣṭakas*: "O Jagadīśa, I do not desire wealth, or offspring, or a beautiful woman, nor poetical genius, but that from birth to birth spontaneous *bhakti* be in me toward you."[35]

These devotional principles contributed to an elaborate ethical model which animated both ascetic (*vairāgin*) communities and lay congregations, creating a strong impact on society. The diffusion of the Gauḍīya movement was uniquely "protestant" in nature in that it laid down roots without a stringent hierarchical structure. Associations of Vaiṣṇava "brotherhoods" were established that were called *parivāra* (family). A strong sense of belonging, tempered by a sense of freedom from caste dictates were key elements in the rapid expansion of early Gauḍīya Vaiṣṇavism.[36]

Most of the Gauḍīya traditions accept nine propositions as collated in the work of an eighteenth-century theologian,

Baladeva Vidyābhūṣana. His Sanskrit treatise, the *Prameya-rātnavalī*, may be derivative of another work that was originally attributed to Madhva (ca. 1238-1317 C.E.), the founder of a Vaiṣṇava dualistic tradition (*dvaita-vedānta*). In any case, the nine points were meant to provide readers with precise theological guidelines, as follows:

1. God is the highest substance.
2. He is known through all the revelations.
3. The world is real.
4. The differences are real.
5. The souls are real.
6. There are various grades of souls.
7. Release is the attainment of god.
8. Its cause is the worship of god.
9. Proofs are three: perception, inference, and authority.[37]

The enumeration is revered as an authoritative doctrinal canon. Notice that it assigns supremacy to Kṛṣṇa, the source of all godly descents (*avatāra*).[38] The revealed scriptures, according to Baladeva, are the means for knowing god; they are subdivided according to a three-fold model[39] whereby some sections deserve special emphasis. For instance, the *Bhāgavata-purāṇa* should be consulted to reconcile conflicting statements that appear in other scriptures.[40] The world, according to Baladeva's interpretation of the scriptures, is constituted of divine energy which is real, although the world is temporary. The soul is eternally distinct from divinity; moreover, no form of ultimate union with eternity is admitted since this would preclude servitude to god, the highest possible achievement.[41] There are differences among individual souls (*jīva*) because of past deeds (*saṃskāra*) and present practices (*sādhana*). Liberation is not so much an escape from the cycle of rebirth as the achievement of an attitude (*bhāva*) of pure and selfless service to god (*preman*).[42] God is to be known—or experienced—along a path of devotion (*bhakti-mārga*) that is monitored by three guardians: direct perception, deductive reasoning, and scriptural authority, the accepted model of apprehension according to classical Indian theories of knowledge.[43]

## DOCTRINAL ASPECTS PECULIAR TO ISKCON

Gauḍīya theology is no doubt sophisticated, as its detailed treatment filling countless pages of Sanskrit, Hindi, and Bengali works would suggest. This library was added to by Bhaktivedānta himself, who was a prolific and tireless author, and by his disciples as they researched their wide heritage to pen additional volumes in settling controversial issues.[44]

However, there is another theology that constitutes a "popular," everyday approach to religion and is easier to summarize. It is this simpler version of the theology that nourishes faith in most ISKCON believers. Most devotees would acknowledge the intricacies explicated above, but in their daily lives, the complex, scholarly approach is less compelling than a simple belief in Kṛṣṇa as the center of their tradition and the supreme god (*parama-īśvara*) and in a life arranged around him. They consider themselves to be Kṛṣṇa's servants (*nitya-dāsa*), and they conceive of human life as an opportunity to revive their devotion to and surrender to god. The ancestral forgetfulness of the eternal relationship with god began with a descent from the spiritual world to our temporary and illusory world; to remove this oblivion, a devotee who has received the grace of his guru, Kṛṣṇa's representative, ought to engage steadfastly in chanting the holy names and in performing devotional service.

These practices are directed toward two complementary goals. On one hand, the devotee tries to free himself from the coils of material illusion and mundane attachments, and on the other hand, through his devotion, he attempts to attract the attention of Kṛṣṇa, the only one who can bestow the final liberation from the cycle of rebirth (*saṃsāra*) and bring the soul back to the spiritual realm.

The typical life project of an ISKCON believer is eloquently expressed in Bhaktivedānta's introduction to the *Bhagavad-gītā*: "Of course everyone has a particular relationship with the Lord, and that relationship is evoked by the perfection of devotional service. But in the present status of our life, not only have we forgotten the Supreme Lord, but we have forgotten our eternal relationship with the Lord."[45]

If one asks a member of ISKCON what the essential tenets of their beliefs are, the answer generally involves three fundamental issues: Who are we? Where do we come from? Where do we go? Devotees consider their doctrine to be sufficient to address these three vital questions.

The answer to the first item is entailed in the following formula: "We are not this material body, but spiritual souls, forgetful of our true eternal nature, which is made of happiness and knowledge." The second question is answered thus: "Somehow or other, having lost our original state of perfection, we fell down in the world of cyclic rebirth. We have already gone through many lives, and we have been covered by many bodies, and from time to time we have been thinking of being trees, fishes, tigers, or lambs; children, elders, men, or women; singing angels or hellish demons; but each time we have eventually left our body which has briefly accompanied us, and we have believed we were dying." The third issue is addressed along these lines: "The bodies taken by us during our cycle of embodied life are imposed on us by the natural law of karma, which punctually rewards us in relation to our conduct during a life and the thoughts we had at the time of death. However, when we want to interrupt this cycle to go back to our original nature, to God's association, we turn to the practice of *bhakti*, loving service to God. Thus, we fully engage our body, mind, and speech, and we try to satisfy our worshipable deity; by his grace, we will finally go back to Kṛṣṇa."[46]

Ritual practices, ethical models, and indeed, every ordinary activity is aimed at the realization of such a reality. The morning liturgy, the prayer, the meditation, and community service all train the thoughts to be in constant remembrance of Kṛṣṇa. Every activity performed within the community, be it cooking, gardening, book sales, or whatever, is offered to god. In this way, the believer surrenders to god all his deeds, his thoughts and words, and moves within a coherent horizon of sense.

ISKCON's theology could be called an ascetic doctrine with a soteriologic background, although not one that precludes lay members, who are not directly involved in community life. The ritualistic routine of each day in the life of a temple resident is founded on a set of rules that is meant to maintain individual and collective purity. One of the most meaningful moments in any Kṛṣṇa devotee's life is the initiation ceremony. It is a moment when the novice makes a commitment to serve god, is ceremonially reborn to a new life, and becomes tied to a mentor in the form of an initiating master.

Thus, the ISKCON believer, while agreeing with most of the Gauḍīya doctrinal versions delineated above, sums them up in a more concise salvation doctrine aimed at devotional practice and finalized in the purification of the soul, which is thought to be the only requirement in achieving the ultimate goal of life: love of god (*kṛṣṇa-preman*).

# 4.

# Directions, Developments, and Areas of Controversy

In the 1990s ISKCON leaders resolved to accept the responsibility for past errors and for many problems that continue to hamper the smooth flow of the movement's activities. It was a courageous act that reflected sincere soul-searching and a serious attempt at renewal. Currently, it provides much of the impetus for future initiatives, and some of the issues that once plagued the movement are now under scrutiny. Before responsibility could be claimed, the first step was to recognize that the problems existed. In the early years, members seemed blinded to the sometimes unpleasant social circumstances they found themselves in.

With the aim of renewal, the Governing Body Commission, during its annual meeting in 1993, promoted a world questionnaire to gauge the members' status and their day-to-day realities vis-a-vis the organization. The greater goal was to heal, to weld and strengthen the collective identity of the movement.[1] A respected scholar who had written about ISKCON, Burke Rochford, was asked to conduct the survey under the heading "Prabhupāda Centennial Survey."

The decision to confront issues is attested to in the opening lines of a document dating from the late 1990s:

> As the Governing Body Commission concluded at its 1996 special meeting in Abentheuer, [Germany], "ISKCON's house is on fire." The movement faces serious social problems. Devotees are dissatisfied, confused about their responsibilities and hampered in achieving their full potentials. Everyone is suffering, leaders as well as rank-and-file. Women, children and cows are unprotected and abused. Many who for years dedicated themselves to preaching and devotional service are now outsiders. Others are "hanging on" with diminishing hope of finding a secure, decent life in ISKCON. Others, who should be free to be models of renunciation and spiritual leadership, are perceived to be entangled with money and power.[2]

Although the impulse to change was not unequivocal or unanimous, the initiatives were an earnest attempt to solve real problems and to usher in a new era of development. ISKCON had long been operating on an international scale, and the dynamic strength of such a movement made the need to address social issues even more compelling. In fact, this need topped the list of priorities that emerged from the survey. After Rochford reviewed responses from more than 2,000 members in fifty-three countries, he outlined the following conclusions, which are liberally paraphrased here:

a. There is a striking lack of trust between ISKCON members and the movement's leadership, as well as among devotees themselves.

b. ISKCON suffers from poor management, and leaders are not always responsive to those they serve.

c. There is a lack of employment opportunity within ISKCON.

d. The educational alternatives within ISKCON are inadequate.

e. The (mis)treatment of women within the movement has negatively affected women's sense of self-esteem and limited their ability to make spiritual progress.
f. Of critical importance to the stability of ISKCON has been the erosion of traditional religious authority in the face of scandal and controversy involving ISKCON's gurus and *saṇnyāsins*.
g. Related to the demise of religious authority has been the apparent decline of Governing Body Commission authority among some portions of ISKCON's membership.[3]

These issues continue today to be some of the most sensitive difficulties. The difference now is that the leadership seems to be focused on how to resolve these problems, however painful the process may be. Lay members, too, have organized private initiatives to address such topics.

In this regard, the role of the second generation is proving to be important. The remarks of an ISKCON representative at a public conference in Germany are an example:

> The affair has also prompted more and more of ISKCON's members to consider the social integration of Vaishnavism into German society a high priority. Consequently, open discussion and reassessment of social and philosophical issues have become the norm among ISKCON's members ... Almost all of ISKCON Germany's management is staffed by second generation members. The guru and *sannyāsa* disciples of Śrīla Prabhupāda, ISKCON's founder, are withdrawing from these positions, and it is expected that in the future they will be responsible only for their individual missionary projects. This is a significant development, as the second generation's perspective on social integration differs greatly from that of the first generation. For instance, the push for the Wiesbaden conference and the initiatives for dialogue

with scholars and church representatives came from second generation members."[4]

As promising as such goals are, it should be noted that the achievements of the founding generation were not insignificant, among which the following should be mentioned: the distribution of free vegetarian food in many underdeveloped areas of the world, the large-scale diffusion of ethical and theological principles contained in the *Bhagavad-gītā* and other scriptures, the acquisition of impressive estates in almost every country and the construction of temples, and the diffusion of Bhaktivedānta's writings on a scale of 500 million copies distributed thus far.

It is also important to note the progress relative to ISKCON's sense of belonging. During the 1990s the "moderate" type of devotee gained ground so that adherents are no longer confined to monastic communities. Indeed, they now often live in middle-class suburbs and are employed in ordinary jobs. Lay people have new rights as ISKCON members, although still along a nuanced spectrum of membership. Yet, this development checked the wave of desertions that characterized the 1980s. Even in the 1980s, a person's departure did not necessarily imply abjuration of belief, but rather the need to find a suitable social position. The new attitude is more flexible and welcoming and will certainly help stabilize ISKCON's membership.

As far as the bond between individuals and the institution is concerned, this will no doubt continue to evolve as members reassess the once lofty models that were held up for their emulation in favor of more realistic examples that can be harmonized with their own life experiences. Claims of superiority that some leaders have made in comparing ISKCON and its members to the larger society are being made with less frequency. The institution seems more fully committed to accommodating those who seek a spiritual dimension to their lives but not to the exclusion of every other interest. In the future, one can expect to see the establishment of general lay congregations in acknowledgment of the population shift. One might also predict an increased role in education, religious instruction for children, and counseling as the organization ceases to be the intractable and infallible stronghold of charisma.[5]

## EDUCATION AND NEW HORIZONS FOR YOUTH INDOCTRINATION

ISKCON has sometimes seen itself as being first and foremost an educational institution to instruct people in spiritual matters. This is an emphasis that can be traced to the teachings of Bhaktivedānta himself, as well as to the writings of other ISKCON scholars and believers. Lately, it has become the position of those who see this as the only feasible path in the wake of the demise of communal living.[6]

In the early 1970s, Bhaktivedānta promoted an ambitious educational scheme that would provide an alternative upbringing from primary school to the advanced grades for ISKCON children. Gradually, schools were opened, but over time, the changes that transformed the movement as a whole affected the schools as well. There were two purposes for the schools: the need to provide parochial education for a growing number of children of devotees and, out of a transcendental-utopian necessity, to create a class of individuals *(brāhmaṇa)* who would be capable of directing humanity in spiritual matters.

The first of these *gurukulas* ("school of the guru") was inaugurated in Dallas in 1971. After some ups and downs, it encountered an impasse with local authorities and eventually closed in 1974. Two new schools were opened in 1975 in New Vṛndāvana, West Virginia, and in Los Angeles. A short time later, a large *gurukula* was opened in Vṛndāvana, India. The *gurukulas* continued to multiply until, by 1978, there were a dozen in the United States alone. New schools were later opened in Australia, England, Italy, and France.[7] In 1983 there were sixteen *gurukulas* in industrial countries and seven in developing countries,[8] all of them boarding schools, or rather, "residential schools" (*aśrama-gurukula*). The founder's expectations for the *gurukula* system were being realized as he entrusted young students to the care of devotees whose emphasis was on ethical and spiritual development. Unfortunately, the teachers were not as committed to academic or practical training.[9]

Despite the seriousness of the original intent behind the schools, the last two American *gurukulas* closed at the end of 1986 in conjunction with the collapse of the community model and the overall institutional crisis. In Italy and France, the schools were closed in the early 1990s. A few survived, and the large *gurukulas* in Māyāpur and Vṛndāvana (India) have continued to operate.[10] Among the other issues that contributed to the schools' demise, the fact that students suffered from an identity complex and alienation and found few employment opportunities when they graduated just compounded the situation. These issues continue to affect the movement's progress and public image.

With the decline of the *gurukulas,* the student population disappeared from the communities, along with their parents. The leaders were forced to find new proselytizing and pedagogic strategies, which in turn prompted the shift in attention from temple communities to the outlying congregations.

Education and upbringing remain worrisome for ISKCON,

but leaders have come to see these as tools instead of obstacles to increasing the membership and consolidating and stabilizing the movement.[11] ISKCON has appointed commissions to study adult education, including graduate-level programs, and to arrange for accreditation. A significant development was the founding, through independent initiative, of a handful of prestigious institutions of higher education including the Oxford Centre for Vaiṣṇava and Hindu Studies, an impressive center located near England's most prestigious university; the Institute for Vaiṣṇava Studies in Berkeley, California; the Vaiṣṇava Training Education centers in London and Oxford; and similar centers in India and elsewhere. Even though these institutes operate more-or-less independently of the GBC, they reflect an important cultural development for ISKCON. Beginning in 1994, the staff of the Vaiṣṇava Training Education centers have served as traveling tutors for ISKCON communities to help train novices and to address some of the needs of the general membership.

ISKCON has recently promoted cultural activities aimed at establishing a dialogue with representatives and members of other creeds[12] and with some of the most notable scholars of the Christian world.[13] The scope and potential of these meetings have prompted enough interest among the GBC for it to appoint a committee to explicitly endorse and express its views on inter-religious dialogue.[14]

## THE TIMELESSNESS OF CONTROVERSY

Some observers assume that as ISKCON continues to develop, and as its roots deepen, the conflicts and controversies it experienced in the formative years will dissipate. As an expanding religion with an international presence, such a view is probably misguided. In fact, as the structure of an institution broadens over the course of time, as religious doctrines become more systematized and orthodoxy is established—indeed, as the bureaucracy grows—the gap between the status quo and minority opinions widens and managers come to be seen as less representative of, and responsive to, the rank-and-file—all of which heightens rather than decreases tensions and ruptures.

ISKCON is confronted with various contemporary challenges, both from within and without. The disputed issues include legal controversies regarding the copyright of Bhaktivedānta's works; questions about the quality of the editing of his writings;[15] the legitimacy of his successors; the unfortunate ongoing risk of gurus betraying their vows; a conspiracy theory that the founder died by poisoning; and a power struggle among many Indian gurus who, according to ISKCON, exploit the advantage of belonging to a tradition akin to Bhaktivedānta's.

ISKCON endeavors to distinguish itself from its cousin organizations and thereby raises the problem of "denominationalism."[16] The predicament is that there is no longer a unique and unequivocal representation of a true Hare Kṛṣṇa devotee. Each believer, in his or her own unique way, refers to one of the multifaceted denominations and is, at the same time, connected to a shared heritage. Simultaneously, ISKCON's quarrel with the anti-cult movement has not ended. The anti-cult activists have troubled ISKCON around the world since the early 1970s, defaming ISKCON's leaders with charges of moral laxity, brainwashing, and other misdeeds.[17] These organizations have had a huge impact on ISKCON's public image, as indicted by recent problems for ISKCON Europe when the census was commissioned by the European Parliament.[18]

After thirty years of hostility, one of the most influential anti-cult organizations in the United States, the American Family Foundation, recently invited representatives of ISKCON to its annual convention. During a workshop, ISKCON representatives were respectfully listened to as they explained their points of view.[19]

The event offered a glimmer of hope for future encounters that may be as serene and fruitful. The outlook is indeed promising.

A carved stone statue of the Hindu god Viṣṇu from the Chennakeśava Temple, A.D. 1117, in Belur, India.

Bhaktivinoda Ṭhākura (1838-1914), deputy magistrate for the district of Jagannātha Purī (shown here in his judicial robes), temple supervisor, intellectual, and guru.

Bhaktisiddhānta Sarasvatī, shown here preaching, ca. 1933. He was Bhaktivinoda Ṭhākura's son, mentor to ISKCON's founder.

Abhay Caran De (seated left), founder of ISKCON, before taking his vows. His wife is standing behind him, his father is seated in the center, and he holds his son in his lap.

The *sannyāsa* initiation in 1959 when Bhaktivedānta officially became a *svāmin*. Bhaktivedānta is on the right and his *sannyāsa* guru is seated in the center.

Bhaktivedānta presenting a copy of the *Śrīmad-Bhāgavatam* to the president of India, Lal Bahadur Shastri, ca. 1962.

Bhaktivedānta with Sumati Morarji, head of the Scindia Steamship Company, who gave Bhaktivedānta free passage from India to New York in 1965.

"Swamiji," as Bhaktivedānta was known to his followers, shown here in the courtyard behind his storefront temple on Second Avenue in Manhattan.

Bhaktivedānta alone in New York in the 1960s.

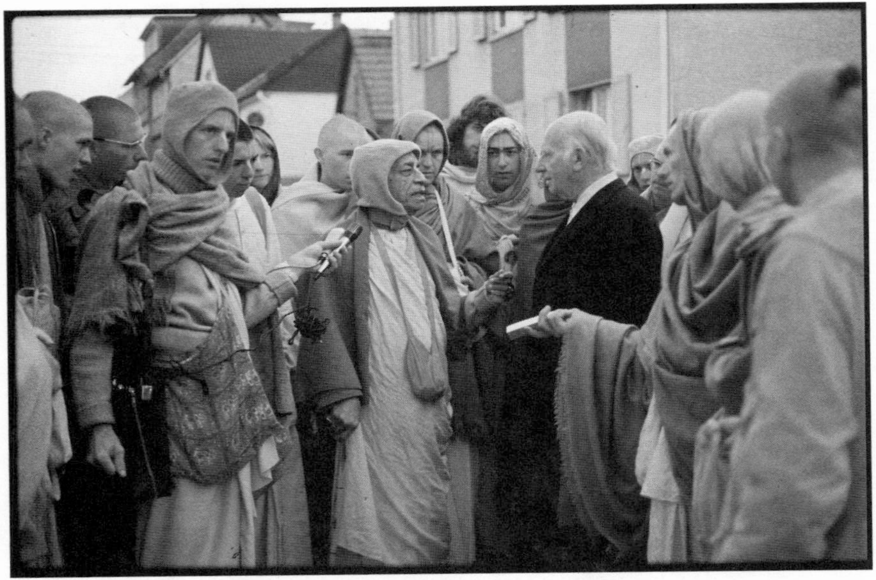

Bhaktivedānta, ca. 1974, on a morning walk discussing philosophy with prominent German philosopher Emile Durckheim.

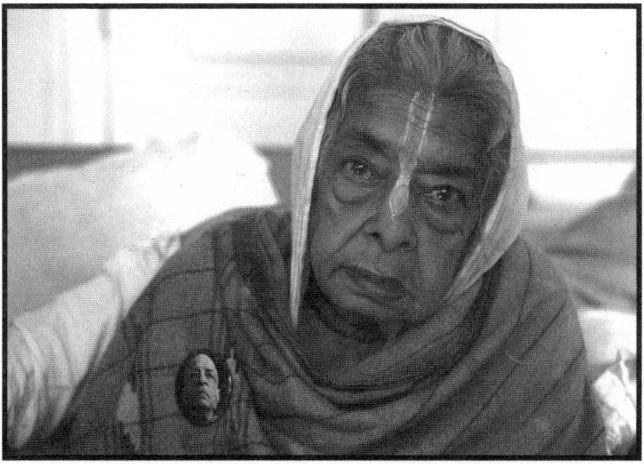

Pisima, sister of Bhaktivedānta and devotee of Kṛṣṇa.

The New York Rathayatra Cart Festival on Fifth Avenue, an annual ISKCON event in Manhattan and other cities around the world.

Satsvarūpa Dāsa Gosvāmī, one of the eleven original *zonal ācāryas* and official biographer of Bhaktivedānta.

Bhaktivedānta on a morning walk, during which he would engage disciples in theological discussions.

Bhaktivedānta enjoying the moment on the grounds of Bhaktivedānta Manor near London, 1973.

The Los Angeles temple, known as ISKCON's "Western World Headquarters," ca. 1972.

The ISKCON world headquarters in Māyāpur, West Bengal. This group photograph was taken in 1976.

The Kṛṣṇa Balarām Temple in Vṛindāvana—one of several ISKCON temples in India. This image was captured when the temple was newly completed in 1975.

Bhaktivedānta at a Rathayatra Festival held in Balboa Park in San Diego, 1975.

Disciples sitting on the lawn at Bhaktivedānta Manor outside London, 1973.

Caitanya and Nityānanda deity statues in ISKCON's Zurich temple.

# Notes

## Chapter 1. History

1. Hereafter, with diacritical marks, as Hare Kṛṣṇa.

2. Thomas J. Hopkins, "Why Should ISKCON Study Its Own History?" *ISKCON Communications Journal* 6 (Dec. 1998): 1-6; Hopkins, "An Addendum to: Why Should ISKCON Study Its Own History?" *ISKCON Communications Journal* 7 (June 1999): 69-70.

3. When ISKCON's proselytizing effort was at its height in the mid-1970s, there were about 5,000 resident members throughout the world, although most were in the United States. After the founder's death, the focus of activity shifted to Asian countries, especially India, and to European countries.

4. Burke Rochford researched a sample of almost 2,000 subjects worldwide and addressed the problem of the repartition of the analysis units and of the spheres of belonging. See his "Prabhupāda Centennial Survey: A Summary of the Final Report," *ISKCON Communications Journal* 7 (June 1999): 16.

5. Burke Rochford, "Demons, Karmies, and Non-Devotees: Culture, Group Boundaries, and the Development of Hare Kṛṣṇa in North America and Europe," *Social Compass* 47 (June 2000): 169-186.

6. Burke Rochford, "Family Formation: Culture and Change in the Hare Kṛṣṇa Movement," *ISKCON Communications Journal* 5 (Dec. 1997): 74-75.

7. Rāsamaṇḍala Dāsa, "An Analysis of ISKCON Membership in the United Kingdom: Moving into Phase Three," *ISKCON Communications Journal* 3 (Dec. 1995): 84-85; Eugenio Fizzotti, et al., "Appartenenza al Movimento Hare Krishna e Profili di Person-

alità: Indagine in una Comunità Italiana," *Orientamenti Pedagogici* 44/4 (1997): 768-776.

8. For samples, see the United States where in 2000 there were 750-900 residents of forty-five ISKCON centers, with 50,000-70,000 sympathizers of varying degrees of belonging and participation.

9. On the life of Bhaktivedānta, see Satsvarūpa Gosvāmī, *Śrīla Prabhupāda Līlāmṛta*, 6 vols. (Los Angeles: Bhaktivedānta Book Trust, 1980-1984). See also the "ISKCON/A. C. Bhaktivedānta Svāmī" issue of the *Journal of Vaiṣṇava Studies* 6 (spring 1998).

10. The thoughts and teachings of Gauḍīya Vaiṣṇava masters were the central subject of Bhaktivedānta's preaching, especially the currents inspired by Caitanya Mahāprabhu, who lived in Bengal at the turn of the sixteenth century (1486-1533). On the history of the Gauḍīya Vaiṣṇava, see Edward C. Dimock and Tony K. Stewart, eds., *Caitanya-caritāmṛta of Kṛṣṇadāsa Kavirāja: A Translation and Commentary,* Harvard Oriental Series vol. 56 (Cambridge, MA: Harvard University Press, 1999), 3-25; Sushil Kumar De, *Early History of the Vaiṣṇava Faith and Movement in Bengal* (Calcutta: Firma KLM, 1961); Melville T. Kennedy, *The Chaitanya Movement: A Study of the Vaiṣṇava of Bengal* (Delhi: Munshiram Manoharlal, 1993); Edward C. Dimock, *The Place of the Hidden Moon: Erotic Mysticism in the Vaiṣṇava Sahajiyā Cult of Bengal* (Chicago: University of Chicago Press, 1989); David L. Haberman, *Acting as a Way of Salvation: A Study of Rāgānugā Bhakti Sādhana* (New York City: Oxford University Press, 1988); Anjali N. Chatterjee, *Sri Krsna Caitanya: An Historical Prospective* (Delhi: Associated Publishing Company, 1984).

11. Satsvarūpa, *Śrīla Prabhupāda Līlāmṛta,* 1:32-33.

12. On the life of Bhaktisiddhānta Sarasvatī, see Rūpa Vilāsa Dāsa, *A Ray of Viṣṇu* (Washington, MS: New Jaipur Press, 1988).

13. Caitanya Mahāprabhu (1486-1533) was born in Bengal and became the original promoter of Gauḍīya Vaiṣṇavism.

14. An ancient hymn traceable to *Ṛg-veda*, 3.62.10. On the *gāyatrī mantra* in Vaiṣṇava traditions, see Guy L. Beck, "Variation on a Vedic Theme: The Divine Names in the Gāyatrī Mantra," *Journal of Vaiṣṇava Studies* 2 (spring 1994): 47-58.

15. See chapter 2 of this volume for initiation rites.

16. For a classical view of brahmanic life, see Patrick Olivelle, *Rules and Regulations of Brahmanical Asceticism* (Albany: State University of New York, 1995), and Olivelle's *The Aśrama System: The History and Hermeneutics of a Religious Institution* (New York City: Oxford University Press, 1993). For pedagogic models in literary contexts, vedic and post-vedic, see Radha Kumud Mookerji, *Ancient Indian Education: Brahmanical and Buddhist* (Delhi: Motilal Banarsidass, rpt. 1998).

17. The reform character of Bhaktisiddhānta's teachings followed the lead of his father, Bhaktivinoda Ṭhākura (1838-1914). See Shukavak N. Dāsa, *Hindu Encounter with Modernity* (Los Angeles: SRI Publications, 1999); Rūpa Vilāsa, *The Seventh Gosvāmī* (Washington, MS: New Jaipur Press, 1989).

18. Satsvarūpa, *Śrīla Prabhupāda Līlāmṛta,* 1:90-97.

19. Ibid., 92.

20. The magazine is available in a bound volume, *Back to Godhead, 1944-1960: The Pioneer Years* (Los Angeles: Bhaktivedānta Book Trust, 1996).

21. Several Indian masters had already helped diffuse Hindu *dharma* oversees out of a nationalist impulse. On the philosophical motives of neo-Hindu movements, and on modern traditionalist movements in India, see the eloquent treatise by Wilhelm Halbfass, *India and Europe* (Delhi: Motilal Banarsidass, 1990), 217-246. See also Gerald James Larson, *India's Agony over Religion* (Albany: State University of New York, 1995), 178-277.

22. His original translation is available digitally on the *Bhaktivedānta VedaBase,* ver. 4.11 (Sandy Ridge, NC: Bhaktivedānta Archives, 1999).

23. His travel diary is available as Bhaktivedānta Svāmī, *The Jaladuta Diary* (Los Angeles: Bhaktivedānta Book Trust, 1995).

24. The connection between ISKCON and the 1960s youth movement is discussed in Stillson Judah, *Hare Krishna and the Counterculture* (New York City: John Wiley & Sons, 1974); Jack Moody, *Ethic and Counter Culture: An Analysis of the Ethic of Hare Krishna,* Ph.D. diss., Claremont Graduate School, 1978; J. Gordon Melton, "The Attitude of the Americans toward Hinduism," *Krishna Consciousness in the West,* eds. David Bromley and Larry

D. Shinn (Lewisburg, PA: Bucknell University Press, 1989), 79-100.

25. This was expressed in the "prophetic" poem "Mārkine Bhāgavata-dharma" composed by Bhaktivedānta on Sept. 18, 1965, upon his arrival in Boston (Bhaktivedānta, *The Jaladuta Diary*, 72-74).

26. *The Beginning: The 1966 Journal of His Divine Grace A. C. Bhaktivedānta Swami Prabhupāda* (Los Angeles: Bhaktivedānta Archives, 1998), 65, entry for Feb. 11, 1966.

27. Ibid., 82, entry for Mar. 6, 1966.

28. Satsvarūpa Gosvāmī, *With Śrīla Prabhupāda in the Early Days, 1966-1969* (Port Royal, PA: Gita Nagari Press, 1991), 1-81.

29. The registration papers and related documents were recently published in *The Beginning*, op. cit., 50-55.

30. Bruce Scharf and Steven Rosen, "1965: It Was a Very Good Year," *Journal of Vaiṣṇava Studies* 6 (spring 1998): 43-59; Francine Daner, *The American Children of Krishna* (New York City: Rinehart and Winston, 1976).

31. The theologian Harvey Cox discusses the receptive climate at the time in Steven Gelberg, ed., *Hare Krishna, Hare Krishna: Five Distinguished Scholars on the Krishna Movement in the West* (New York City: Grove Press, 1983), 40-44.

32. This derives from an ancient festival held annually in Jagannāth, India, in which Jagannātha, an effigy of Kṛṣṇa, is carried through the streets and publicly worshiped.

33. Satsvarūpa Gosvāmī, *Prabhupāda-Līlā* (Potomac, MD: Gita Nagari Press, 1987), 77-79.

34. This motto was first used in Bhaktivedānta Svāmī to Mukunda, 18 Feb. 1968. Hereafter all references to Bhaktivedānta's correspondence are from the *Bhaktivedānta VedaBase*, op. cit.

35. On the early success, see Burke Rochford, *Hare Krishna in America* (New Brunswick, NJ: Rutgers University Press, rpt. 1991); Larry D. Shinn, *The Dark Lord: Cult Images and the Hare Krishnas in America* (Philadelphia: Westminster Press, 1987).

36. The role of social customs in inventing a new life is dealt with in Shinn, *The Dark Lord*, 97-121.

37. Beginning in March 1975, this committee met for an annual plenary session in the grand complex in Māyāpur, West Ben-

gal. These meetings are held in parliamentary fashion, as introduced by Bhaktivedānta himself at the first annual meeting in 1975 when he raised his hand to vote as any other member, thus setting the example. Proposals that are accepted by the majority of GBC members become permanent "resolutions," binding for all ISKCON members.

38. Today the Bhaktivedānta Book Trust owns copyrights for all of Bhaktivedānta's writings and oversees their publication in several languages.

39. Governing Body Commission (hereafter GBC), *Resolution 1*, Mar. 9, 1976. See also Bhaktivedānta to Śrī Govinda, Dec. 25, 1972; to Dāmodara, Aug. 1, 1973; to Rāmeśvara, Jan. 1, 1975; to Ajita, Jan. 6, 1975; to Rūpānuga, Jan. 9, 1975; to Kīrtānananda, Oct. 15, 1976.

40. Satsvarūpa, *Śrīla Prabhupāda Līlāmṛta*, 4:111-114; Tamāl Kṛṣṇa Gosvāmī, "The Perils of Succession: Heresy of Authority and Continuity in the Hare Krishna Movement," *ISKCON Communications Journal*, 5 (June 1997): 19.

41. In several cases disciples of Bhaktivedānta, after initiation and a period of activity in India, came into contact with other masters of the Gauḍīya Maṭha school. This is testified by letters in which Bhaktivedānta warned his disciples to be "very careful about them and not mix with them. This is my instruction to you all." Bhaktivedānta to Rūpānuga, Apr. 28, 1974. See also letters to Pradyumna, Feb. 17, 1968; to Mukunda, Mar. 26, 1968; to Hṛṣīkeśa, Jan. 9, 1969; Jan. 31, 1969; to Rāmeśvara, Oct. 17, 1975; and to Viśvakarma, Nov. 9, 1975.

42. A record of this friction is present in letters between Bhaktivedānta and many of his disciples. Siddhasvarūpa, a disciple of Bhaktivedānta, came to be considered by some as a spiritual alternative to Bhaktivedānta. See Bhaktivedānta to Gaurasundara, Aug. 26, 1972; to Sudevī, 15 Aug. 1972; to Tuṣṭa Kṛṣṇa, 14 Dec. 1972; to Sudama, 10 Apr. 1974; to Manaśvi, 1 Apr. 1975; and to Paramāhaṃṣa, 16 July 1975. The founder also discussed the topic in his Morning Walk in Los Angeles, Jan. 9, 1974.

43. This occurred in 1975-76 and was triggered by some controversial GBC resolutions. See particularly *Resolutions 1-5*, Mar.

9, 1976; also Satsvarūpa, *Śrīla Prabhupāda Līlāmṛta,* 6:166-70; Tamāl, "The Perils of Succession," 29-31.

44. A memo from Bhaktivedānta to all temple presidents on April 8, 1972, reads: "I beg to inform you that recently some of the Governing Body Commission members held a meeting at New York on 25th through 28th March, 1972, and they have sent me a big big minutes, duplicated, for my consideration and approval, but in the meantime they have decided some appointments without consulting me. ... This has very much disturbed me. ... I do not follow exactly what is the motive of the so-called GBC meeting, therefore I have sent the telegram which you will find attached herewith, and I have received the replies as well. Under these circumstances, I AUTHORIZE YOU TO DISREGARD FOR THE TIME BEING ANY DECISION FROM THE GBC MEN UNTIL MY FURTHER INSTRUCTION. ... Finally, I beg to repeat that ALL GBC ORDERS ARE SUSPENDED HEREWITH BY ME UNTIL FURTHER NOTICE" (emphasis in original).

45. For an estimate of book sales, see Rochford, *Hare Krishna in America,* 173-189; Rochford, "Family Formation," 70-73.

46. Bhaktivedānta translated the first nine of twelve cantos—the first canto being a revision, heavily emended and edited, of the Indian version published by Bhaktivedānta from 1962 to 1965 in Delhi—and then worked on the tenth canto, which his disciples completed after his death. Over time, the work was published in several formats, including an eighteen-volume edition. See A. C. Bhaktivedānta, trans., *Śrīmad-bhāgavatam* (Los Angeles: Bhaktivedānta Book Trust, 1999). Collier-Macmillan released Bhaktivedānta's *Bhagavad-gītā* in 1968, and the Bhaktivedānta Book Trust later released its own abridged version as *Bhagavad-gita as It Is: With Translations and Elaborate Purports by Prabhupāda* (New York City: Prabhupāda Book Trust, 1972).

47. Details about his travels are available in Tamāl Kṛṣṇa Gosvāmī, *TKG's Diary: Prabhupāda's Final Days* (Dallas: Pundits Press, 1998).

48. On many occasions Bhaktivedānta said he wanted to entrust his disciples with more administrative and publishing responsibilities, but never suspended his own managerial oversight, partly because of the lack of experience and wavering com-

mitment of his young disciples. See Bhaktivedānta to Rūpānuga, Nov. 30, 1971; to Gaurasundara, Aug. 26, 1972.

49. See Shinn, *The Dark Lord,* 46-60.

50. Thus reads the last testament signed by Bhaktivedānta on June 4, 1977.

51. The letter was co-signed by Bhaktivedānta and his personal secretary, Tamāl Kṛṣṇa Gosvāmī.

52. A "codicil" signed by Bhaktivedānta on Nov. 5, 1977, a few days before his death, emended portions of his last testament dated June 4, 1977.

53. Transcripts of two recorded conversations from May 28 and July 7, 1977, are available, although with a mistaken date for the second conversation, in Rochford, *Hare Krishna in America,* 283-286.

54. The issue of spiritual succession has always attracted enormous attention in ISKCON. A bulky trove of literature has been produced on this theme, both in favor and against the legitimacy of the eleven successors; the transmission of charisma implemented after Bhaktivedānta's disappearance has also been both defended and criticized. The following are some of the texts that fueled the debate: Karnāmṛta Dāsa and Rūpa Vilāsa Dāsa, *Living Still in Sound* (Washington, MS: New Jaipur Press, 1990); anon., *Our Living Guru* (Ukiah, CA: PADA, 1993); anon., *Śrīla Prabhupāda: Our Dīkṣā Guru,* 1994 (available on the VADA online database at *www.harekrsnas.com);* Haṃsaduta Dāsa, *Śrīla Prabhupāda: His Movement and You* (Geyserville, CA: Nam Hatta World Sankirtan Party, 1993); Jayantakrd Dāsa, *Śrī Guru-Tattva* (Treziers, France: n.p., 1994); Steven Gelberg, ed., *The Spiritual Master and the Disciple* (Bombay: Bhaktivedānta Book Trust, 1990); Vīrabahu Dāsa, *The Guru and What Prabhupāda Said* (Los Angeles: Fondo Editorial Bhaktivedanta, 1988); Śivarāma Svāmī, *The Śikṣā-Guru: Implementing Tradition Within* (Budapest: ISKCON Bhaktivedānta Institute, 1999).

55. Larry Shinn wrote interesting profiles of the most prominent of the eleven gurus derived from personal experiences (*The Dark Lord,* 50-60).

56. The possibility of electing new gurus was first examined by the GBC on March 19, 1978 (*Resolution 16*). It was decided to

invest the gurus among the GBC members with this responsibility (cf. *Resolution 1,* Mar. 21, 1978). Known as the Ācārya Committee, the group produced several preliminary documents such as "The Descending Process of Selecting a Spiritual Master," sanctioned by the GBC on March 11, 1981 (*Resolutions 4-5*). Organizational and charismatic oversight were awarded to the committee by the GBC on March 11, 1981 (*Resolution 10.1-6; Resolution 11*).

57. Shinn, *The Dark Lord,* 51; Rochford, *Hare Krishna in America,* 222-23; 227-28; Nori J. Muster, *Betrayal of the Spirit: My Life Behind the Headlines of the Hare Krishna Movement* (Chicago: University of Illinois Press, 1997), 44.

58. Shinn, *The Dark Lord,* 49.

59. GBC, *Resolution 3,* Mar. 18, 1983. The background for this ratification is presented in Muster, *Betrayal of the Spirit,* 44-5; Rochford, *Hare Krishna in America,* 229. In each temple, a *vyasāsana* holds a life-like statue of the founder, called a *murti.*

60. On the master-teacher guru model, the Sanskrit sources are many and varied; a comprehensive summary is out of the question here, but for some of the most meaningful passages, see *Bṛhadāraṇyaka Upaniṣad* IV.1.2-7; *Chāndogya Upaniṣad* II.23.1; IV.5.1; VII.15.1-2; VIII.15.1; *Taittirīya Upaniṣad* I.11.1-2; *Muṇḍaka Upaniṣad* I.2.12; *Mānavadharmaśāstra* II.68-73; II.140-145; II.203-208; II.242-249. The oldest mention of the word guru is in *Chāndogya Upaniṣad* VIII.15.1. For an exhaustive and scholarly analysis of the word, see Jan Gonda, *Change and Continuity in Indian Religion* (Delhi: Munshiram Manoharlal, rpt. 1997), 229-283. The Gauḍīya code on the master-disciple (*guru-śiṣya*) relationship is included in Gopāla Bhaṭṭa Gosvāmī's sixteenth-century *Hari-bhakti Vilāsa*: vilāsa I. Moreover, for an overall survey of the vedic teacher's role, especially regarding initiation, see Rajbali Pandey, *Hindu Saṃskāras* (Delhi: Motilal Banarsidass, 1994), 106-25. ISKCON has its own understanding of the topic (see Sivarāma, *The Śikṣā-Guru,* 81-90).

61. Tamāl, *The Perils of Succession,* 23-24.

62. Shinn, *The Dark Lord,* 55-56; Rochford, *Hare Krishna in America,* 230-33.

63. The tone of reproach is testified to by GBC, *Resolution 16,*

Jan. 25, 1980, when other senior members of ISKCON claimed the right to become gurus. The schisms are dealt with by *Resolution* 22, Feb. 25, 1980.

64. Jan Brzezinski, "The Paramparā Institution in Gauḍīya Vaiṣṇavism, *Journal of Vaiṣṇava Studies* 5 (winter 1997): 163-165. See also Bhaktivedānta to Rūpānuga, Apr. 28, 1974.

65. Shinn, *The Dark Lord,* 59.

66. Ravindra Svarūpa Dāsa, "Cleaning House and Cleaning Hearts: Reform and Renewal in ISKCON, Part Two," *ISKCON Communications Journal* 2 (Dec. 1994): 28. The author relates the modernization of tradition to the process of actualization and reinterpretation begun by Bhaktivinoda Ṭhākura (1838-1914), the father of Bhaktivedānta's master, thus legitimizing the divergence from the Caitanya tradition. This continues to be a subject for disagreement today. On Bhaktivinoda Ṭhākura, see Shukavak's *Hindu Encounter with Modernity,* op. cit, and his "The Kṛṣṇa-Saṃhitā and the Adhunika-Vāda: Ṭhākur Bhaktivinode and the Problem of Modernity," *Journal of Vaiṣṇava Studies* 5 (winter 1997): 127-150. On issues related to the legitimization of change, see Brzezinski, "The Paramparā Institution," 151-82; Tripurāri Svāmī, *Srī Guru-Paramparā* (Mill Valley, CA: Harmonist Publishers, 1998), 16.

67. GBC, *Resolution 2.1-3,* Feb. 27, 1982. In that same context, a decalogue for *guru ācāryas* was also approved; the idea was to institutionalize and contain the figure of the *guru ācārya* within prescribed bounds (see *Resolution 4.I-III,* Mar. 5, 1982).

68. Jayatirtha Svāmī was suspended Mar. 6, 1982, and dismissed Mar. 16, 1983.

69. Rochford, *Hare Krishna in America,* 245-255.

70. Hamsadutta Svāmī was eventually removed from office Mar. 6, 1984.

71. State senators John Kelly and Jackie Vaughn, along with state secretary Kondler, published a senate resolution acknowledging the value of ISKCON's contribution to the community in regard to the Fisher Mansion.

72. GBC, *Resolution 6,* Mar. 17, 1983.

73. *The New York Times,* Apr. 18, 1983, 13.

74. The core reform took place in the United States. This is

not surprising since most of the membership was in the U.S. That the original eleven gurus were American is reflected, to some degree, in their management styles.

75. "Report to the North American Governing Body Commission from the North American Temple Presidents, Regional Secretaries, and Sannyasins," Oct. 12-13, 1984 (unpublished).

76. Kīrtanānanda Svāmī, *On His Order* (Bombay: Bhakti Books, 1987), 1-20. This was in response to a reformist paper titled "Under My Order: Reflection on the Guru in ISKCON," August 1985 (unpublished).

77. GBC, *Resolutions 5-6,* Feb. 27, 1985; *Resolutions 2-3,* Feb. 28, 1985.

78. GBC, *Resolution 6.1-4,* Apr. 1, 1986; *Resolutions 6-7,* Apr. 2, 1986.

79. GBC, *Resolutions,* Mar. 30; *Resolutions*, Apr. 1-4, 1986.

80. After this meeting, one of the eleven gurus printed a booklet that epitomized the reform spirit: Satsvarūpa Gosvāmī, *Guru Reform Notebook* (Washington, D.C.: Gita Nagari Press, 1986).

81. There were visible consequences in the liturgy. The daily worship of the guru was redirected exclusively to the founder, as is the custom in all ISKCON centers today.

82. Ravindra, "Cleaning House," 30; Muster, *Betrayal of the Spirit,* 117-18.

83. See Kīrtanānanda, *On His Order,* op. cit.

84. In Europe, temples were crowded with young believers, most of whom were initiated in the early 1980s and knew little of the succession controversies or the shadows that had dimmed the apparent splendor of some of the gurus.

85. These three were Bhagavān Gosvāmī, Rāmeśvara Svāmī, and Bhavānanda Gosvāmī. The GBC held an emergency meeting in San Diego in August 1986 to discuss the behavior of the latter two and consider the brewing turmoil involving Kīrtanānanda and New Vṛndāvana. Bhavānanda agreed to a resolution suspending him from the role of guru, published September 8, but later held an initiation ceremony and was consequently expelled. In the annual meetings of March 1987, the GBC accepted the official resignations of Bhagavān and Rāmeśvara. On the same occa-

sion, Pañcadraviḍa Svāmī, one of the three gurus appointed in 1982, was expelled over doctrinal disagreements.

86. Kīrtanānanda was expelled from ISKCON, along with his followers, in March 1987. Two years earlier he nearly died from head injuries sustained from a violent assault by one of his acolytes.

87. "Resolution of the Joint Meeting of the North American Temple Presidents and North American Prabhupāda Disciples," Chicago, Nov. 17-18, 1986 (unpublished).

88. GBC, *Resolutions 50-87*, Mar. 1987.

89. As undisputed authorities of their zones, the *guru ācāryas* enjoyed secular and spiritual hegemony with full power over the economic and spiritual destinies of their territories. Being members of the GBC, they could also influence the overall direction of the movement.

90. GBC, *Resolutions 72, 87*, Mar. 1987.

91. This new perspective did not altogether dispel the contradictions and misgivings. If a guru was the only medium between god and man and therefore above judgment, how could he be contained by a hierarchy that was superior to him? On the guru's role in vedic literature, see Gonda, *Change and Continuity*, 229-283.

92. Shinn, *The Dark Lord*, 60.

93. Some of the data about ISKCON's presence in the early 1980s in England can be found in Kim Knott, *My Sweet Lord* (Wellingborough, Northhamptonshire: Aquarian Press, 1986), 44-50.

94. The ISKCON community in Los Angeles was populated by almost four hundred adult members in 1980 and only sixty in 1994. Other large communities in Chicago, New York, and Detroit experienced similar declines.

95. Burke Rochford, "Crescita: Espansione e Mutamento nel Movimento degli Hare Krishna," *Religioni e Sette nel Mondo* 1/1 (1995): 69-72.

96. On the various aspects of the New Vṛndāvana case, see John Hubner and Lindsey Grueson, "Dial Om for Murder," *Rolling Stone*, Apr. 9, 1987, 53-58, 78-82; Michael R. Blake, "Heaven, West Virginia: Legitimation Techniques of the New Vrindaban

Community," in *Krishna Consciousness in the West*, 188-216; Muster, *Betrayal of the Spirit*, 54-60, 159-160.

97. John Hubner and Lindsey Grueson, *Monkey on a Stick: Murder, Madness, and the Hare Krishnas* (San Diego: Harcourt Brace, 1988).

98. Paraphrasing a well-known passage from Caitanya's medieval biography: "Instruct whomsoever you see about Kṛṣṇa; by my command, having become a guru, save this country" (Dimock and Stewart, *Caitanya-caritāmṛta*, madhya-līlā VII.125).

99. As of September 2001, the number of officially authorized gurus was seventy.

100. The *ṛtvik* theory, now officially branded heretical, asserts that a disciple of Bhaktivedānta occupying the guru position does not officiate on his own behalf but acts as an officer "invested of power" by the founder.

101. "Krishna's Followers in Moscow," *Soviet Union Illustrated Monthly*, Dec. 1990, 12.

102. Even today Hindu communities are an important source of support for many ISKCON centers; nonetheless, the link between spiritual assistance and fund raising is not clear. This is noted by Rochford, "Crescita: Espansione e Mutamento," 74-78; Rāsamaṇdala, "An Analysis of ISKCON Membership," 89; Nurit Zaidman, "When the Deities Are Asleep: Processes of Change in an American Hare Krishna Temple," presented at the CESNUR Annual Convention in Rome, 1995.

103. Serge Simon, "Krishnas Find Fertile Ground in Russia," *Chicago Tribune*, Mar. 8, 1992.

104. On ISKCON schools, see Burke Rochford, "Education and Collective Identity: Public Schooling of Hare Krishna Youth," *Children in New Religions*, eds. Susan Palmer and Charles Hardman (New Brunswick, NJ: Rutgers University Press, 1999), 29-50; Burke Rochford and Jennifer Heinlein, "Child Abuse in the Hare Krishna Movement, 1971-1986," *ISKCON Communications Journal* 6 (June 1998): 43-70.

105. ISKCON Communication Europe (ICE) was constituted in 1991 to coordinate public relations efforts in Europe. Today it directly influences the GBC's international development policies while it shepherds ISKCON's public image in Europe, producing

common directives and communication strategies for representatives involved in inter-religious dialogue, media relations, and liaisons with the European Parliament and other international bodies. Since January 1993 ICE has published the biannual magazine *ISKCON Communications Journal,* one of the most respected forums for ISKCON news and self-analysis. ICE is affiliated with the activities of ISKCON Communication Global, an office that has existed for a decade, documented in Mukunda Gosvami's *Inside the Hare Krishna Movement* (Badger, CA: Torchlight Publishing, 2001).

106. The manor is located near a small suburban town, Letchmore Heath, in Hertsmere Borough. In 1981 the borough council heard complaints about traffic to and from the manor, and the issue escalated for over a decade and involved appeals to national and European authorities. Only when a separate freeway access road was constructed, bypassing the town and avoiding any impact on the peace and quiet of its residents, did the issue begin to subside. See Malory Nye, "Hare Krishna and Sanatan Dharma in Britain: The Campaign for Bhaktivedānta Manor," *ISKCON Communications Journal* 4 (June 1996): 5-23.

107. Jaya Śila, et. al, "Seeing Beyond '96: Proceedings of the ISKCON Social Development Conference," 1997, 3.

108. ISKCON's position in India is peculiar and would require a longer treatment than can be offered here. See, e.g., Charles Brooks, *The Hare Krishnas in India* (Princeton, NJ: Princeton University Press, 1989); Brooks, "A Unique Conjecture: The Incorporation of ISKCON in Vrindaban," *Krishna Consciousness in the West,* 165-187.

109. The defectors were Swamis Jagadīśa and Somaka. Later, another four gurus left their offices. The following are the dates of the respective resignation letters: Jagadīśa Svāmī, Oct. 10, 1996; Somaka Svāmī, Dec. 30, 1997; Bhakti Vaidurya Madhava Svāmī, Apr. 23, 1998; Īśvara Svāmī, May 22, 1998; Harikeśa Svāmī, Aug. 13, 1998; and Bhakti Abhay Caran Svāmī, Nov. 10, 1999.

110. On this development, see "The Final Order," Oct. 1996, a document forwarded to a subcommittee of the GBC, which answered it with the paper, "Prabhupad's Order," Aug. 1998.

111. In February 1999 the GBC approved a resolution to ban all

promotion of *ṛtvik* theories. An excerpt from Law 302 begins by quoting the *ISKCON Law Book,* 6.4.7.2, concerning the "posthumous ritvik" doctrine and then explains: "The doctrine that Srila Prabhupada continues to initiate direct *dīkṣa* disciples after his departure from this world through officiating priests (*ṛtviks*) is a dangerous philosophical deviation. It is totally prohibited in ISKCON. No devotee shall participate in such posthumous *ṛtvik* initiation ceremonies in any capacity including acting as *ṛtvik,* initiate, assistant, organizer, or financier. No ISKCON devotee shall advocate or support its practice."

112. This position is clearly expressed in the GBC's "Guru and Initiation," in *ISKCON: Laws of ISKCON* (Māyāpur, West Bengal: GBC Press, 1995); Badrinarayan Dāsa, et. al, "Disciple of My Disciple: An Analysis of the Conversation of May 28, 1977," Mar. 1997 (available on the VADA database at *www.harekrsnas.com.*). See also Śivarāma, *The Śikṣā-Guru.*

113. Many sources attest to Bhaktivedānta's integrity. See Larry D. Shinn, "Reflections on Spiritual Leadership: The Legacy of Śrīla Prabhupāda," *ISKCON Communications Journal* 4 (Dec. 1996): 17-22; Shinn, *The Dark Lord,* 25-42; Charles Selengut, "Charisma and Religious Innovation: Prabhupāda and the Founding of ISKCON," *ISKCON Communications Journal* 4 (Dec. 1996): 51-63; Klaus Klostermaier, "The Education of Human Emotions: Śrīla Prabhupāda as Spiritual Educator," *ISKCON Communications Journal* 4 (June 1996): 25-32.

114. Mark Chaves, "Secularization as Declining Religious Authority," *Social Forces* 72 (Mar. 1994): 756.

115. Max Weber, *Economia e Società* (Milano: Edizioni di Comunità, 1961), 1:238, our own translation. Cf. Luciano Cavalli, *Il Capo Carismatico: Per una Sociologia Weberiana della Leadership* (Bologna: Il Mulino, 1981), 70; Cavalli, *Carisma: La Qualità Straordinaria del Leader* (Roma and Bari: Laterza, 1995), 5.

116. Enzo Pace, *Le Sette* (Bologna: Il Mulino, 1997), 25-33.

117. Rodney Stark, "How New Religions Succeed: A Theoretical Model," *The Future of New Religious Movements,* eds. D. Bromley and Phillip Hammond (Macon, GA: Mercer University Press, 1987), 29.

118. Rochford, "Crescita: Espansione e Mutamento," 76.

119. Federico Squarcini, "In Search of Identity: Memory, Oblivion, and Thought-Style in the Hare Krishna Movement," *Social Compass* 47 (June 2000): 253-271.

120. See, e.g., Rochford, "Crescita: Espansione e Mutamento."

121. The word *saṃkīrtana* is a nominal composition, literally meaning "proper glorification." ISKCON maintains that its meaning is "congregational glorification." Traditionally it was applied to chanting and singing addressed to god, a practice that could be performed either privately or collectively.

122. ISKCON uses *saṃkīrtana* as a synonym for book distribution and fund raising. On this latter usage, see Rochford, "Family Formation," 66; Rochford and Heinlein, "Child Abuse," 51-53, 61; Enzo Pace, "Tempo Sacro e Tempo Sociale nei Movimenti Religiosi Neo-Orientali in Europa," *Il Tempo e il Sacro nelle Società Post-Industriali*, eds. Arnaldo Nesti and Pietro De Marco (Milano: Franco Angeli, 1997), 294-298.

123. Burke Rochford, "Movement and Public in Conflict: Values, Finances, and the Decline of the Hare Krishna Movement," *Money and Power in New Religions*, ed. James Richardson (Lewiston, NY: Edwin Mellen Press, 1987), 271-303; Rochford, "Dialectical Processes in the Development of the Hare Krishna: Tension, Public Definition, and Strategy," in *The Future of New Religious Movements*, 109-122.

124. The emphasis on book distribution was most pronounced leading up to a critical period in ISKCON history, as well as during the 1990s. For representative examples, see Śubhānanda Dāsa, ed., *Preaching Is the Essence* (Los Angeles: Bhaktivedānta Book Trust, 1977); Harikeśa Svāmī, *All Glories to the Saṃkīrtana Devotees* (Korsnas Gard, Sweden: Sentient Press, 1996).

125. For an assessment of ISKCON book distribution, see Rochford, "Family Formation," 70-73.

126. Pace, "Tempo Sacro e Tempo Sociale," 296.

127. Rochford, *Hare Krishna in America*, 224.

128. Rāsamaṇḍala, "An Analysis of ISKCON Membership," 86.

129. Rochford, *Hare Krishna in America*, 230.

130. Shinn, *The Dark Lord*, 13-24.

131. Anson Shupe and David Bromley, *The New Vigilantes: Deprogrammers: Anti-Cultists and the New Religions* (Beverly Hills: Sage

Publications, 1980); Bromley, *The Anti-Cult Movement in America: A Bibliography and Historical Survey* (New York City: Garland, 1984); Shinn, *The Dark Lord,* 164-167; Alessandro Usai, *Profili Penali dei Condizionamenti Psichici: Riflessioni sui Problemi Penali Posti dalla Fenomenologia dei Nuovi Movimenti Religiosi* (Milano: A. Giuffrè, 1996), 32.

CHAPTER 2. PRACTICES AND RITUALS

1. For descriptions of traditional Gauḍīya practices, see Sushil Kumar De, *Early History of the Vaiṣṇava Faith and Movement in Bengal* (Calcutta: Firma KLM, 1961), 408-541; Melville T. Kennedy, *The Chaitanya Movement: A Study of the Vaisnava of Bengal* (Delhi: Munshiram Manoharlal, 1993), 180-216; Edward C. Dimock, *The Place of the Hidden Moon: Erotic Mysticism in the Vaisnava Sahajiya Cult of Bengal* (Chicago: University of Chicago Press, 1989), 181-221; David L. Haberman, *Acting as a Way of Salvation: A Study of Raganuga Bhakti Sadhana* (New York City: Oxford University Press, 1988), 115-144.

2. Particularly interesting is the social network established by ISKCON in its Indian temples and communities. See Charles Brooks, "ISKCON's Place in the Bengal Vaishnava Tradition of Caitanya Mahāprabhu," *Journal of Vaiṣṇava Studies* 6 (spring 1998): 5-30; Brooks, *The Hare Krishnas in India* (Princeton, NJ: Princeton University Press, 1989); Brooks, "A Unique Conjecture: The Incorporation of ISKCON in Vrindaban," in *Krishna Consciousness in the West,* eds. David Bromley and Larry D. Shinn (Lewisburg, PA: Bucknell University Press, 1989), 165-187; Shukavak N. Dāsa, "ISKCON's Link to Sādhana-bhakti within the Caitanya Vaishnava Tradition," *Journal of Vaiṣṇava Studies* 6 (spring 1998): 189-212.

3. On the variegation, mutability, conflict, and dynamism of Indian religious traditions, see Jan C. Heesterman, *The Inner Conflict of Tradition: Essays in Indian Ritual, Kingship, and Society* (Chicago: University of Chicago Press, 1985); Wilhelm Halbfass, *Tradition and Reflection: Exploration in Indian Thought* (Albany: State University of New York, 1991); Gerald James Larson, *In-*

*dia's Agony over Religion* (Albany: State University of New York, 1995).

4. The information conveyed here is drawn partly from the canonic manual, *Pāñcarātra-Pradīpa,* 2 vols. (Mayapur, India: ISKCON GBC Press, 1994).

5. The analysis of Indologist Rahul Peter Das is of particular interest (Rahul, "'Vedic' in the Terminology of Prabhupāda and His Followers," *Journal of Vaiṣṇava Studies* 6 (spring 1998): 141-159. On the connection between ISKCON and other Gauḍīya traditions, see Rahul, *Essays on Vaiṣṇavism in Bengal* (Calcutta: Firma KLM, 1997), 54-71.

6. Statues of marble or brass are found in Hindu temples as images of divinity, known as *mūrtis* in Sanskrit, and are specific to each tradition. They are installed in the sancta sanctorum with a grand ceremony called *pratiṣṭhā* (installation), which is when their "divinization" takes place.

7. Ancient Indian sources mention three styles of *jāpa*: loud, murmured, and silent (mental). In ISKCON the first is viewed as superior because it allows others to hear god's holy names and benefits everyone rather than just the individual chanter. Traditionalists maintain that silent *jāpa* is best because it involves utter concentration and is thus more thoroughly pure. For an example of the traditional view, see *Mānavadharmaśāstra* 2.85.

8. This implies the repetition of a Sanskrit *mantra* sixteen times for each of the 108 beads of the rosary. The *mantra* comes from *Kali-santarana Upanisad* 1.2: *hare rāma hare rāma rāma rāma hare hare / hare kṛṣṇa hare kṛṣṇa kṛṣṇa kṛṣṇa hare hare / iti ṣoḍaśakaṃ nāmnāṃ kali-kalmaṣa nāśanam / nātaḥ parataropayaḥ sarva vedeṣu dṛśyate.* On the underlying theology, see Norvin J. Hein, "Caitanya's Ecstasies and the Theology of the Name," in *Hinduism: New Essays in the History of Religions,* ed. Larry Smith (Leiden, Netherlands: E. J. Brill, 1976), 16-32. For a traditional view, see Raghava Caitanya, *The Divine Name* (Berhampur, India: Bhakti Vigyan Nityananda Book Trust, rpt. 1997).

9. The theological motives for this emphasis are described in Guy L. Beck, *Sonic Theology: Hinduism and Sacred Sound* (Columbia: University of South Carolina, 1993), 183-203.

10. Tamāl Kṛṣṇa Gosvāmī, "The Dance of the Dexterous Her-

meneute: Transformation vs. Continuity, Tension in Scriptural Transmission," *Journal of Vaiṣṇava Studies* 6 (spring 1998): 61-72.

11. Regarding Bhaktivedānta's commentary on the *Bhagavad-gītā*, see the apologetic text written by Śivarāma Svāmī, *The Bhaktivedānta Purports: Perfect Explanation of the Bhagavad-gītā* (Badger, CA: Torchlight Publishing, 1998). For an intriguing critique of the founder's approach to the *Bhagavad-gītā*, cf. Eric Sharpe, *The Universal Gītā: Western Images of the Bhagavad Gītā* (LaSalle, IL: Open Court, 1985), 141-147.

12. Burke Rochford, "Family Formation: Culture and Change in the Hare Krishna Movement," *ISKCON Communications Journal* 5 (Dec. 1997): 68-72; Rochford. "Crescita: Espansione e Mutamento nel Movimento degli Hare Krishna," *Religioni e Sette nel Mondo* 1/1 (1995): 75-78.

13. ISKCON has a complex set of norms that guide the master-disciple relationship. For details, see "Gurus and Initiation in ISKCON: Law of the International Society for Krishna Consciousness," 1996 (unpublished).

14. The initiation procedure is, in some ways, peculiar and exclusive to ISKCON. In older Gauḍīya Vaiṣṇava traditions, there were separate ceremonies and practices for *vaiṣṇava-dīkṣā*. One of these included five sanctifying elements known as *pañca-saṃskāra*: the guru marked the adept's body with sacred symbols (*tāpa*), he applied the vertical *tilaka* mark (*urdhva-puṇḍra*), bestowed on him a new name (*nāma*), introduced the disciple to prayer and revealed the sacred stanzas (*mantra*) to him, and initiated him to ritual worship (*yāga*). This procedure is described by the Gauḍīya Vaiṣṇava theologian Baladeva Vidyābhūṣaṇa (*Prameya-ratnāvalī* VIII.1-12). A description of a canonical Gauḍīya initiation rite is included in an older work (Gopāla Bhaṭṭa Gosvāmī, *Hari Bhakti Vilāsa*, vilāsa II). For a comparison with vedic and post-vedic models of initiation (*dīkṣā*), see Jan Gonda, *Change and Continuity in Indian Religion* (Delhi: Munshiram Manoharlal, rpt. 1997), 315-462; Rajbali Pandey, *Hindu Saṃskāras* (Delhi: Motilal Banarsidass, 1994), 106-152.

15. Lecture of Bhaktivedānta Svāmī on *Śrīmad-Bhāgavatam*, December 12, 1970. Besides meat, fish and eggs are forbidden.

16. On the standard enforced for ISKCON celibates and ministers, see one of the early manuals, *Hare Kṛṣṇa Handbook* (Los Angeles: Bhaktivedānta Book Trust, 1970), 44-52.

17. For brahminic initiation customs in ancient India, see, e.g., *Mānavadharmaśāstra* II.36-44.

18. A long composite thread (*upavīta*) in cotton or silk is draped from the left shoulder to the right hip as the distinctive mark of the brāhmanas (the priestly class) and, in classical times, also of warriors and merchants. For an instructive historical perspective on the ancient use of the *yajñopavīta*, see Pandurang Vaman Kane, *History of Dharmaśāstra* (Pune, India: Bhandarkar Oriental Research Institute, rpt. 1997), 2.1:287-297.

19. Guy L. Beck, "Variation on a Vedic Theme: The Divine Names in the Gayatri Mantra," *Journal of Vaisnava Studies* 2/2 (1994): 47-58.

20. The investiture of the sacred thread is sometimes called *upanayana*. The history and meaning of the word are not clear or linear. See Kane, *History of Dharmaśāstra*, 268-334; Pandey, *Hindu Saṃskāras*, 115-116.

21. Manuals with standardized ceremonies and liturgies have been published that attempt to make sense of the contemporary extrapolations of ancient rites and intricacies of deity worship. See ISKCON's *Pāñcarātra Pradīpa;* Prema Rasa Dāsa, *The Book of Saṃskāras: Purificatory Rituals for Successful Life* (Los Angeles: Bhaktivedanta Book Trust, 1998).

## Chapter 3. Doctrine and Theology

1. Gauḍa is the ancient name of the region corresponding to a good portion of today's Bengal.

2. On the Vaiṣṇava currents in medieval India, see Narendra Nath Bhattacharyya, ed., *Medieval Bhakti Movements in India* (Delhi: Munshiram Manoharlal, rpt. 1999); Edward C. Dimock, *The Place of the Hidden Moon: Erotic Mysticism in the Vaisnava Sahajiya Cult of Bengal* (Chicago: University of Chicago Press, 1989), 41-67.

3. On the Gauḍīya doctrines, see Sushil Kumar De, *Early History of the Vaiṣṇava Faith and Movement in Bengal* (Calcutta:

Firma KLM, 1961), 225-447; Melville T. Kennedy, *The Chaitanya Movement: A Study of the Vaisnava of Bengal* (Delhi: Munshiram Manoharlal, 1993), 88-122; Rahul Peter Das, *Essays on Vaiṣṇavism in Bengal* (Calcutta: Firma KLM, 1997), 23-38.

4. On Ṭhākura Bhaktivinoda's life, see Shukavak N. Dāsa, *Hindu Encounter with Modernity* (Los Angeles: SRI Publications, 1999); Rūpa Vilāsa Dāsa, *The Seventh Gosvāmī* (Washington, MS: New Jaipur Press, 1989).

5. On Bhaktisiddhānta's life, see Rūpa Vilāsa Dāsa, *A Ray of Viṣṇu* (Washington, MS: New Jaipur Press, 1988).

6. On this multi-faceted change of perspective, see Shukavak, *Hindu Encounter with Modernity;* Shukavak N. Dāsa, "The Kṛṣṇa-Saṃhitā and the Ādhunika-vāda: Ṭhākur Bhaktivinode and the Problem of Modernity," *Journal of Vaiṣṇava Studies* 5 (winter 1997): 127-150; Jan Brzezinski, "The Paramparā Institution in Gauḍīya Vaiṣṇavism," *Journal of Vaiṣṇava Studies* 5 (winter 1997): 151-182.

7. The need to adapt the doctrine to changing times is emphasized in a recent paper by one of ISKCON's leading intellectuals: Ravīndra Svarūpa Dāsa, in "ISKCON and Varṇāśrama-Dharma: A Mission Unfulfilled," *ISKCON Communications Journal* 7 (June 1999): 35; also Jan Brzezinski, "What Was Śrīla Prabhupāda's Position: The Hare Kṛṣṇa Movement and Hinduism," *ISKCON Communications Journal* 6 (Dec. 1998): 27-50.

8. Shukavak N. Dāsa, "ISKCON's Link to Sādhana-bhakti within the Caitanya Vaishnava Tradition," *Journal of Vaiṣṇava Studies* 6 (spring 1998): 189-212; Charles Brooks, "ISKCON's Place in the Bengal Vaishnava Tradition of Caitanya Mahāprabhu," *Journal of Vaiṣṇava Studies* 6 (spring 1998): 5-30; Brooks, *The Hare Krishnas in India* (Princeton, NJ: Princeton University Press, 1989).

9. Jan C. Heesterman, *The Inner Conflict of Tradition: Essays in Indian Ritual, Kingship, and Society* (Chicago: University of Chicago Press, 1985); Wilhelm Halbfass, *Tradition and Reflection: Exploration in Indian Thought* (Albany: State University of New York, 1991).

10. On the historical and doctrinal differences, see Sushil, *Early History of the Vaiṣṇava Faith,* 1-33; Edward C. Dimock and

Tony K. Stewart, eds., *Caitanya-caritāmṛta of Kṛṣṇadāsa Kavirāja: A Translation and Commentary*, Harvard Oriental Series, vol. 56 (Cambridge, MA: Harvard University Press, 1999), 10-25; 107-141.

11. On Caitanya's life and biographical sources, see Dimock and Stewart, *Caitanya-caritāmṛta,* 82-98; Prabhat Mukherjee, *History of the Caitanya Faith in Orissa* (Delhi: Manohar Publications, 1979), 1-10; Oudh Bihari L. Kapoor, *The Philosophy and Religion of Sri Caitanya* (Delhi: Munshiram Manoharlal, 1977), 57-61; Joseph T. O'Connell, "Historicity in the Biographies of Caitanya," *Journal of Vaiṣṇava Studies* 1 (winter 1993): 102-132.

12 *Bhāgavata-purāna* XI.5.32; Kavirāja, *Caitanya-caritāmṛta,* ādi-līlā I, śloka 1-5; madhya-līlā XIX, śloka 3; antya-līlā XX, śloka 2.

13. Rahul, *Essays on Vaiṣṇavism,* 23-38.

14. Dimock and Stewart, *Caitanya-caritāmṛta,* 10.

15. Traditionally there are only eight stanzas, called *śikṣāṣṭaka* ("the eight teachings"), that can be ascribed to Caitanya, initially recorded by Rūpa Gosvāmī in his work, *Padyavālī.* Cf. Sushil Kumar De, ed., *The Padyāvalī: An Anthology of Vaiṣṇava Verses in Sanskrit* (Delhi: Navrang, rpt. 1990), śloka 22; 31-32; 71; 93-94; 324; 337. The eight stanzas appear in a collated version in Kavirāja, *Caitanya caritāmṛta,* antya-līlā. XX, śloka 3-10. See ibid., antya-līlā XX.9-38 for Kavirāja's comments on the *śikṣāṣṭaka.*

16. On the historicity of Jīva, a *gosvāmī* and prolific author, see Tarapada Mukherjee and John C. Wright, "An Early Testamentary Document in Sanskrit," *Bulletin of SOAS,* School of Oriental and African Studies, University of London, Vol. XLII, Part 2, 1979.

17. The main references are two famous "notebooks" in Bengali known as *kaḍacā,* ascribed to Murāri Gupta and Svarūpa Dāmodara, who were contemporaries and close associates of Caitanya; the latter's notebook is now lost. The authenticity of another ancient *kaḍacā,* attributed to Govindadāsa Karmakāra, is questioned and it is not accepted by Gauḍīya orthodoxy.

18. On the works of Caitanya's followers, see Sushil, *Early History of the Vaiṣṇava Faith,* 556-672; Kennedy, *The Chaitanya Movement,* 123-147. Interesting details about the flourishing lit-

erary environment of the times are available in Dusan Zbavitel, *Bengali Literature* (Wiesbaden, Germany: Harrassowitz, 1976), 124-198; Kumar Chatterji, "Letteratura Bengali," *Le Civiltà dell'-Oriente*, ed. Giuseppe Tucci, vol. II. (Rome: Gherardo Casini Editore, 1957), 662-668.

19. Alan W. Entwistle, "Vaiṣṇava Tilakas," *IAVRI Bulletin* (International Association of the Vrindaban Research Institute) 11-12 (1981-1982): 49.

20. Zbavitel, *Bengali Literature*, 180-181.

21. Shukavak, "ISKCON's Link to Sādhana-bhakti," 189-212.

22. This tenet is generally demonstrated by quoting the *Bhāgavata-purāṇa* 1.3.28, "But Kṛṣṇa is god himself," in line with traditional Gauḍīya theology. The stanza is one of the central pillars of Jiva Gosvāmī's better known work, *Kṛṣṇa-sandarbha* I.1-50.

23. Kavirāja, *Caitanya-caritāmṛta*, madhya-līlā VI.143-150; VIII.116-125; XX.101-104.

24. *Bhagavad-gītā* IV.4-6; from J. A. B. van Buitenen, ed., *The Bhagavadgītā in the Mahābhārata* (Chicago: University of Chicago Press, 1981). See also *Bhagavad-gītā* XIII.14-16; XV.13.

25. Kavirāja, *Caitanya-caritāmṛta*, ādi-līlā VII.114-126; madhya-līlā VI.154.

26. Ibid., madhya-līlā XXII.57.

27. This spiritual yearning is expressed in the last of Caitanya's *śikṣāṣṭaka*, which reads: "He may crush my breasts in embracing me, a slave to his feet, he may destroy my heart by not appearing to me, he may be a libertine wherever he wants, but still he is the lord of my heart, and there is no other" (ibid., antya-līlā XX, śloka 10).

28. *Bhāgavata-purāṇa* XI.3.21. The guru is regarded by Gauḍīyas as no different than god. Cf. Kavirāja, *Caitanya-caritāmṛta*, ādi-līlā I.15; I.27; I.29. Furthermore, discipleship (*gurupādāśraya*) is listed as the first necessary step in devotional practice (*sādhana-bhakti*) in Rūpa Gosvāmī, *Bhakti-rasāmṛta-sindhu* I.2.74.

29. Denominationalism also applies to the Gauḍīya world; i.e., from a common canon different interpretations are derived, and consequently, many denomination are created. See David L. Haberman, *Acting as a Way of Salvation: A Study of Raganuga*

*Bhakti Sadhana* (New York City: Oxford University Press, 1988), 94-114; Peter, *Essays on Vaiṣṇavism*, 23-38.

30. The issues are the nature of *bhakti*, its availability to individuals, and the role of god and his energies in the world. Gauḍīya theology speaks of internal, marginal, and external energies (*svarūpa-śakti, taṭasthā-śakti, bahiraṅga-śakti*). See Kavirāja, *Caitanya-caritāmṛta*, madhya-līlā VI.143-149; VIII.116-123; XX.101-104; XXII.55-59; Jīva Gosvāmī, *Tattva-sandarbha* 33.1-3. About the autonomous nature of *bhakti*, see Rūpa Gosvāmī, *Bhakti-rasāmṛta-sindhu* I.1.11; I.2.2-4. On the guru's role in bestowing *bhakti*, see Kavirāja, *Caitanya-caritāmṛta*, madhya-līlā XIX.133-134; XV.117.

31. For an overall view, see Arthur L. Herman, *The Problem of Evil and Indian Thought* (Delhi: Motilal Banarsidass, 1993); Wendy Doniger O'Flaherty, *The Origin of Evil in Hindū Mithology* (Berkeley: University of California Press, 1976). On the various understandings of *karman*, classic and non-classic, see O'Flaherty, ed., *Karma and Rebirth in Classical Indian Traditions* (Berkeley: University of California Press, 1980).

32. Kavirāja, *Caitanya-caritāmṛta*, ādi-līlā III.31; VII.9; XVII.19.

33. "*kīrtanīyaḥ sadā hariḥ,*" ibid., antya-līlā XX (last line of the third *śikṣāṣṭaka*).

34. Rūpa, *Bhakti-rasāmṛta-sindhu* I.4.15-16.

35. Dimock and Stewart, *Caitanya-caritāmṛta*, antya-līlā XX, śloka 6.

36. On this phenomenon, see Aloka Lahiri, *Chaitanya Movement in Eastern India* (Calcutta: Punthi Pustak, 1993), 142-47; Mukherjee, *History of the Caitanya Faith*, 80-87; Surajit Sinha, "Vaiṣṇava Influence on a Tribal Culture," in *Krishna: Myths, Rites, and Attitudes*, ed. Milton Singer (Chicago: University of Chicago Press, 1966), 64-89; Kennedy, *The Chaitanya Movement*, 52-59; Anjali N. Chatterjee, *Sri Krsna Caitanya: An Historical Prospective* (Delhi: Associated Publishing Company, 1984), 157-173. A more general discussion is in Joseph T. O'Connell, "Chaitanya Vaishnava Movement: Symbolic Means of Institutionalization," in *Organizational and Institutional Aspects of Indian Religious Movements*, ed. O'Connell (Shimla, India: Indian Institute of Advanced Study, 1999), 215-239.

37. The list draws its incipient words from the nine chapters of Baladeva Vidyābhūṣaṇa's *Prameya-ratnāvalī*, available as an appendix to Rai Bahadur S. Chandra Vasu, *The Vedānta Sūtras of Bādarāyana with the Commentary of Baladeva* (Delhi: Oriental Books Reprint Corporation, 1979).

38. *Bhāgavata-purāṇa* I. 3.28.

39. For a classical conception of this model, see *Mānavadharmaśāstra* 2.1-15; 12.105-115.

40. The traditional Gauḍīya understanding and arrangement of the entire corpus of Indian scriptures is described in Jīva Gosvāmī, *Tattva-sandarbha*, 11-17, including the preeminence of the *Bhāgavata-purāṇa*, 18-24. On this exegetical debate, see Sushil, *Early History of the Vaiṣṇava Faith*, 225-228.

41. Kavirāja, *Caitanya-caritāmṛta*, antya-līlā XX, śloka 6.

42. The climax of total devotion, even at the price of one's well being, is expressed by Caitanya in the last *śikṣāṣṭaka*. See ibid., antya-līlā XX, śloka 10; also Rūpa, *Bhakti-rasāmṛta-sindhu* I.2.293- 309.

43. *Bhāgavata-purāṇa* X.48.19; XI.13.33.

44. An example is a treatise on the origin of the soul compiled by a committee to assert ISKCON's official position on this issue. See *Our Original Position* (Māyāpur, India: ISKCON Governing Body Commission Press, 1996).

45. Bhaktivedānta Svāmī, *Bhagavad-gītā as It Is* (Sydney: The Bhaktivedānta Book Trust, 1986), 5.

46. Liberally excerpted from an unpublished collection of interviews with ISKCON "non-resident believers."

### Chapter 4. Directions, Developments, and Areas of Controversy

1. Government Body Commission, *Resolution 50*, Feb. 7-21, 1993 (hereafter GBC).

2. *Social Development Report* (ISKCON Commission for Social Development, 1998), 1.

3. cf. Burke Rochford, "Prabhupāda Centennial Survey: A Summary of the Final Report," *ISKCON Communications Journal* 7 (June 1999): 17-19.

4. Arcanā Dāsī, "Thirty Years of ISKCON in Germany: Integration and Reform," *ISKCON Communications Journal* 7 (June 1999): 32.

5. As suggested by one of the leaders in concluding his article: Ravindra Svarupa Dāsa, "ISKCON and Varṇāśrama-Dharma: A Mission Unfulfilled," *ISKCON Communications Journal* 7 (June 1999): 44.

6. On the topic of adult and advanced education, see Akhandādhi Dāsa, "Vaiṣṇava Training and Education," *ISKCON Communications Journal* 2 (January 1994): 67-74; Rasamaṇḍala Dāsa, "An Analysis of ISKCON Membership in the United Kingdom: Moving into Phase Three," *ISKCON Communications Journal* 3 (Dec. 1995): 83-92; Klaus Klostermaier, "The Education of Human Emotions: Srila Prabhupada as Spiritual Educator," *ISKCON Communications Journal* 4 (June 1996): 25-32, 52.

7. The historical and institutional profile of ISKCON schools is sketched in Burke Rochford, "Education and Collective Identity: Public Schooling of Hare Kṛṣṇa Youth," *Children in New Religions,* eds. Susan Palmer and Charles Hardman (New Brunswick, NJ: Rutgers University Press, 1999), 29-50; Rochford and Jennifer Heinlein, "Child Abuse in the Hare Krishna Movement, 1971-1986," *ISKCON Communications Journal* 6 (June 1998): 43-70.

8. GBC, *Resolution 12,* Mar. 18, 1983.

9. For readings on ISKCON schools and the view that they should be formative and doctrinal, see Bhūrijana Dāsa, *The Art of Teaching: A Guide for Training Our Children in Kṛṣṇa Consciousness* (Vṛndāvana: VIHE Publications, 1995).

10. The conflicts connected with ISKCON's residential schools are reported in Rochford and Heinlein, "Child Abuse in the Hare Krishna Movement," 43-70.

11. Among the experts consulted by the leadership, see Sefton Davies, "Education and ISKCON: Some Reflections from an Interested Observer," *ISKCON Communications Journal* 5 (June 1997): 5-11.

12. This is not new to ISKCON. See John A. Saliba, S.J., "The New Religious Movements: Some Theological Reflections," *Horizons* 6/1 (1979): 113-118; and "The Christian Church and the New Religious Movements: Toward Theological Understand-

ing," *Theological Studies* 43 (1982): 468-485; Rose Kenneth, "Has ISKCON Anything to Offer Christianity Theologically?" *ISKCON Review* 2 (1986): 40-51; S. Gelberg. "The Catholic Church and the Hare Krishna Movement: An Invitation to Dialogue," *ISKCON Review* 2 (1986): 60-71. ISKCON Communication directors established guidelines for interreligious practices. See, e.g., Śaunaka Ṛṣi Dāsa, "ISKCON in Relation to People of Faith in God," *ISKCON Communications Journal* 7 (June 1999):1-9.

13. Conferences have been held in Wales (January 1996), Massachusetts (September 1996), and Washington, D.C. (April 1998). The following accounts are all subtitled "A Vaiṣṇava-Christian Conference": Kenneth Cracknell, "The Nature of the Self," *ISKCON Communications Journal* 4 (June 1996): 77-82; Francis X. Clooney, "The Destiny of the Soul," *ISKCON Communications Journal* 4 (Dec. 1996): 71-73; Judson Trapnell, "The Everlasting Soul," *ISKCON Communications Journal* 6 (June 1998): 91-93.

14. Ṛṣi, "ISKCON in Relation to People of Faith in God."

15. ISKCON's editorial division replied to the accusations with *Responsible Publishing: Why and How the BBT Publishes Revisions of Śrīla Prabhupāda's Books* (Los Angeles: Bhaktivedānta Book Trust, 1998).

16. ISKCON has clearly evolved through a denominational phase. See "Interview with Thomas J. Hopkins" in *Hare Krishna, Hare Krishna: Five Distinguished Scholars on the Krishna Movement in the West*, ed. Steven Gelberg (New York City: Grove Press, 1983), 151-157.

17. On the disputes between anti-sect activists and ISKCON, see David Bromley, "Hare Krishna and the Anti-Cult Movement," in *Krishna Consciousness in the West*, eds. David Bromley and Larry D. Shinn (Lewisburg, PA: Bucknell University Press, 1989), 255-292; Larry D. Shinn, *The Dark Lord: Cult Images and the Hare Krishnas in America* (Philadelphia: Westminster Press, 1987), 164-167; Thomas Robbins, "Kṛṣṇa and Culture: Cultural Exclusivity and the Debate over 'Mind Control,'" *ISKCON Communications Journal* 5 (June 1997): 77-84. On the phenomenon of anti-cult movements, see Anson Shupe and David Bromley, *The New Vigilantes: Deprogrammers, Anti-Cultists, and the New Religions*

(Beverly Hills: Sage Publications, 1980); Bromley, *The Anti-Cult Movement in America: A Bibliography and Historical Survey* (New York City: Garland Publishing, 1984).

18. Massimo Introvigne, "Religious Liberty in Western Europe," *ISKCON Communications Journal* 5 (Dec. 1997): 37-48. See also Introvigne and Giovanni Cantoni, *Libertà Religiosa: "Sette" e "Diritto di Persecuzione"* (Piacenza, Italy: Cristianità, 1996), 119-126.

19. "Can Cultic Groups Change: The case of ISKCON," panel discussion, Annual Conference of the American Family Foundation, St. Paul, Minnesota, 14-16 May 1999 (unpublished).

# Further Readings

When exploring a new topic and facing the vast number of books available to choose from, one can feel overwhelmed, although not in the case of ISKCON where there is a frustrating scarcity of sources. Some early standards are still in print, but beyond that, readers will not find a plethora of extensive studies and fresh approaches to the topic.

For current trends, the best sources are the academic journals and some of the in-house ISKCON publications. The modest scholarly output on the part of ISKCON watchers is partly due to the fact that ISKCON is young and of limited scope, with much left for future researchers to consider.

The early groundbreaking works are: Stillson Judah, *Hare Krishna and the Counterculture* (New York: John Wiley & Sons, 1974); Francine Daner, *The American Children of Krishna: A Study of the Hare Krishna Movement* (New York: Holt, Rinehart, and Wiston: 1976); Larry D. Shinn, *The Dark Lord: Cult Images and the Hare Krishnas in America* (Philadelphia: Westminster Press, 1987); and Burke Rochford, *Hare Krishna in America* (New Brunswick: Rutgers University Press, rpt. 1991). These works are invaluable, not only as reference books, but as memorable narratives with sensible and heartfelt observations.

Among the more recent publications, there are two that are especially noteworthy. The international magazine for the sociology of religion, *Social Compass,* produced a special monograph edition of issue 47:2 (2000) devoted entirely to ISKCON with contributors who are among the most highly respected international scholars and experts on the topic. A forthcoming book by Burke

Rochford should be similarly thorough: *Family, Culture, and Secularization in the Hare Krishna.*

The bi-annual English-language publication out of Europe, *ISKCON Communications Journal,* fills a unique niche within the field of ISKCON scholarship. By browsing the table of contents and the well-known names of scholars and observers of ISKCON, one senses the breadth and ambition of the publication, and the thematic approach is convenient for both readers and scholars.

The founder of ISKCON left a prodigious body of work in the form of translations of Hindu classics. From the large reservoir of Sanskrit, Bengali, and Hindi literature, he selected what he felt would be the most useful and authoritative theological and doctrinal resources and translated them into English. They have since been translated into other languages. His primary offerings were: (1) the *Bhāgavata-purāṇa* (also known as *Srīmad-Bhāgavatam*), a *purāṇa* that, because it is largely devoted to describing and praising Kṛṣṇa's character, is especially revered among Gauḍīyas; (2) the *Caitanya Caritāmṛta,* Caitanya's biography; (3) the *Bhakti-rasāmṛta-sindhu,* compiled by Rūpa Gosvāmī, a direct follower of Caitanya; and (4) the *Bhagavad-gītā,* the celebrated Hindu scripture on which many post-Christian readings of *sanātana-dharma* are based.

A fully searchable digital version of all of Svāmī Bhaktivedānta's works, including his correspondence, public lectures, and conversations, is available from ISKCON's archives as: *Bhaktivedānta VedaBase Ver. 4.11* (Sandy Ridge, N.C.: Bhaktivedānta Archives, 1999).

With the rise of the Internet, ISKCON's presence in cyberspace has become ever more prominent, as have the websites of its detractors and competitors. A good browser will locate thousands of relevant sites, but the following are worth noting. The main, official ISKCON site, which also has links to related websites, is http://www.iskcon.org; the website of the Governing Body Commission has information about the individuals who comprise the leadership and current operational matters at http://www.gbc.org.

ISKCON's publishing house, Bhaktivedānta Book Trust, lists all of Bhaktivedānta's works, as well as the most recent ISKCON publications, at http://www.bbt.com. The magazine, *Back to Godhead,* is at http://www.krishna.com. The website of the communications department of ISKCON Europe includes essays and scientific research at http://www.icj.iskcon.net. Similarly, other ISKCON departments have their own specific sites. For instance, the worldwide Food for Life project is at http://www.ffl.com.

## About the Series Editor

Massimo Inrovigne is the managing director of the Center for Studies on New Religions (CESNUR), a network of international academic organizations devoted to the study of emerging religious/spiritual movements. An attorney in private practice in Torino, Italy, he has taught courses and seminars at several academic institutions on the sociology and history of new religions. Additionally, he is the author or editor of some forty books and numerous articles and chapters on the same topic.